ESCAPE FROM THE STEEL COCOON
Accepting My Homosexuality
by
Jeremy Simmons

Authors Choice Press
San Jose New York Lincoln Shanghai

Escape From the Steel Cocoon
Acceptance of My Homosexuality

Authors Choice Press
an imprint of iUniverse.com, Inc.

For information address:
iUniverse.com, Inc.
5220 S 16th, Ste. 200
Lincoln, NE 68512
www.iuniverse.com

Originally published by self

ISBN: 0-595-16363-7

Printed in the United States of America

This book is dedicated
to Russ and Susan

PREFACE

For the purpose of writing this book, my name is Jeremy Simmons. I am a thirty-five-year-old real estate broker who lives and works in Chicago. I am also a homosexual.

I am using the name Jeremy Simmons rather than my own name in order to spare my family any embarrassment, harrassment and criticism from some of their more narrow-minded friends and business associates. Also, I wish to prevent any repercussions from my own friends, relatives and acquaintances, some of whom I mention in this book.

I have taken twenty years to sort out all the factors which shaped my sexual and psychological development. Now, after two years of mulling over my findings, I am relating my discoveries for all readers, both gay and non-gay. In this book, I have examined my life, with all of its positive and negative aspects. I have done so in an effort to encourage readers to compare their own lives to mine, and to see the similarities between us. We have common strengths and weaknesses. Underneath it all, human beings are not that different.

Simply because homosexuals sleep with members of the same sex does not necessarily mean that we are less human or less valuable people than heterosexuals. We gays work at the same jobs, watch the same television shows, shop at the same stores and pay higher taxes than our married counterparts, just like our heterosexual neighbors.

A number of homosexuals and heterosexuals feel that members of the alternate lifestyle are their sworn enemies. Straights, when affecting an air of superiority (i. e., the majority has the Divine Right to rule), or when displaying exaggerated swaggeringly macho behavior, are repugnant to some homosexuals. Conversely, many non-gays find the openly effeminate behavior of some male homosexuals to be offensive.

Numerous heterosexuals who believe the myth that *all* members of the gay community are highly promiscuous feel that this supposed licentiousness is a very disagreeable trait.

The fact is that both communities have theories about life that are well worth sharing. A vow by either community to automatically discount or ignore the ideas and opinions of the other camp limits the world's growth. Such lack of communication destroys all chances for the cohesive and productive collaboration that can be attained by persons of differing lifestyles, when they cooperate with each other. Such prejudiced thinking further separates the two communities, and perpetuates the fears, myths and misunderstandings that keep people alienated from each other. Human potential is universal. Only through open communication can members of varying lifestyles achieve peace, understanding, tolerance, and finally *acceptance* of each other.

This book has been written in the hope that it may reduce the amount of homophobia and heterophobia among those people who fear the unknown elements in each other's lives. Perhaps the beginning is a bridge of understanding that can be built when everyone realizes that all mankind shares a common humanity.

CHAPTER 1

The Beginning: From Egg to Larva

I am the third of three sons, born of an upper middle class family. My ancestors date back to the early 1800's in Chicago. My family is considered to be one of the premier members of Chicago's social register. We are conservative Republicans who, for generations, have helped in our city's growth. Many of today's landmark buildings that grace Chicago's skyline were built by my grandfather Simmons.

The allure of my family's tradition in helping to develop Chicago's architecture and to shape its business community was irresistible to me. I became the fourth generation of real estate brokers in my family. Tradition is of the utmost importance to me. I knew from the time I was eight years old that I wanted to be in the real estate business. As a child, I was allowed by my father to join him during his Saturday appointments showing property. I tingled with excitement at meeting the wide variety of my father's clients. That stimulation has not left me today in the career I most happily pursue. I believe my job is as much an integral part of me as is my sexual orientation.

My father and I are very close today, although we no longer work together. Our growing closer began in 1971, when we joined forces in our family-owned real estate firm, which was later dissolved in 1981.

My father was raised to believe in Duty, Honor, Obedience, Service and Devotion (to God and family). His demeanor is Victorian, and he raised his children to be proper as well. My father never questioned his parents, and he always did as he was told. He expected his children to act the same way. My father wanted to pursue a career in the theatre after graduation from Yale in 1935. He told his parents on Graduation Day that he had a job lined up in New York City. "Don't be an ass!" my grandfather snarled. "There's a desk waiting for you at our Chicago offices. Report there in two weeks!" My father did not argue. He obeyed his father and pursued a successful career in real estate for nearly fifty years.

My father did have an escape mechanism from the office pressures, when they became too great or when he felt frustrated by his father in business. Dad also pursued a most successful and rewarding career for twenty-five years in the Navy Reserve. He retired with the rank of Captain. To this day, my father loves anything nautical. He has many friends in the military, and he is a member of two retired military fraternal organizations. Dad served his country well in the second World War and in Korea. He has a number of commendations from the Navy for his services.

Real estate became a lucrative career for my father as well. He supported his wife and children quite comfortably. I met many of my father's clients, some of whom are still good friends of his. Only as an adult, I realized my father's devotion to his two careers, to his wife, and to his children.

As a youngster, I felt neglected and rejected by my father, except when we spent time together on his Saturday morning appointments. I never told my father of my feelings. I felt it was unmanly to complain. I kept silent about the school activities my parents never attended. I also never openly lamented the fact that my father would not ever work with me on my handicraft projects, which I loved doing. I suffered my loneliness silently, and worked by myself in the basement on projects (such as building a robot using spare pieces of metal and cloth). I also attended sporting events at school alone. I never invited my mother to attend these functions at home or at school without my father being present. Somehow, I did not value her presence as much as I did his. Besides, Mom was busy playing tennis or bridge with her friends, so I had a convenient excuse not to invite her. My mother was also very active on women's boards of two Chicago charities related to child care and adoption. Mom was very active hostessing or attending parties with my father as well. In fairness to my mother, I am sure today that she would have rearranged her schedule had I invited her to attend school functions. She loved me, but I did not love her or appreciate her company.

When I was a teenager, my father approached me, out of the blue, to confess his awareness of his parental neglect of me as a child. "I noticed you making that robot in the basement. I'm sure you wanted me there to help you, but I was too busy trying to make a living. I thought that job came first. Now I know I was wrong. Can you forgive me?"

"No problem, Dad," I said. I was deeply touched by my father's sensitivity and genuine concern for me.

When I was in my early thirties, my father and I discussed the way he raised me and my brothers. Dad related his insecurities about his raising a family. He wanted to do a good job of raising us, but he was afraid that he did not know enough about parenting to do it well. He felt rejected by his father and dominated by his mother. Dad did not want to make the same mistakes his parents had made. He decided to allow Mom and the nurse to do the job. Dad admitted that he distanced himself emotionally from his children. Because I was interested in real estate, Dad jumped at the chance to take me along on his Saturday morning appointments. The business activities we shared became the one avenue Dad would allow himself in attempting to get close to me. We both loved the time we spent together. My brothers were not interested in real estate, so they spent even less time with Dad than I did as a child.

My parents often socialized, which left both my brothers and me at home with our nurse. In later years, we made our own social arrangements with our friends. This ongoing pattern of separatism (adults apart from the children) allowed the three sons to become self-sufficient. In my case, I learned to survive by my own wits. We were growing up, despite our parents' physical absence and lack of guidance.

In those days, my parents were becoming estranged from each other, though they now love each other very much. They have been married for over forty-five years, although not all of those years were consummately happy ones. In the 1960's, I sensed that my parents might divorce. They often fought, drank heavily in each other's presence, sometimes took separate vacations, and slept in separate bedrooms. I suspect they stayed together for the sake of the three of us, their sons. They never discussed their differences in front of me or my brothers, but we could intuitively feel the tension and hostility between our parents at the dinner table or in the living room.

One especially painful incident took place that affected the entire family. My older brother, Mark, and I noticed that our mother was getting very drunk before dinner every night. Mark and I commented to each other how Mom only had two drinks (that we saw) before dinner, but she could still barely talk or eat at the table. Secretly, Mark and I both decided to place a faint pencil mark on our mother's bottle of Scotch. In less than a week, we realized that Mom was consuming a fifth of Scotch every two days! Our father would simultaneously drink four or five Martinis before dinner. Then he had two or three glasses of wine during his meal. Mark and I confronted our parents at dinner one night. We voiced our awareness of the amount of alcohol both our parents were consuming on a regular basis. Mark and I revealed that we had been marking Mom's Scotch bottle and measuring her daily intake. Dad was visibly stunned by the news of how much his wife was drinking. Mom was extremely embarrassed about being caught, but she instantly admitted that our findings were accurate. That evening's agonized discussion permanently ended my mother's secret drinking. Mark and I pleaded with our parents to stop their drinking. Our parents reduced their drinking in our presence, then drinking openly only during the evening hours.

I was ten and Mark was twelve on that fateful night when we took our parents to task about the steady and dramatic increase in their consumption of alcohol. I wonder, now, if they realized back then the level of their own addiction to this form of substance abuse. My parents were raised in an era when "sociable people" were expected to smoke and drink heavily. I felt hurt and angry that my parents drank as much as they did. They have known from the first time Mark and I confronted them until this very day that I do not like their drinking habits. Their excessive dependence on alcohol keeps me away from them emotionally.

In 1980, my mother's doctor told her that she had to stop drinking hard liquor. It was affecting her diverticulitis. She switched to wine, and has reduced her consumption of that substance to a more tolerable level, in my estimation. My father drinks Martinis or Scotch year-round, except during Lent. For the first time that I can remember, Dad suggested during the Lenten season of 1984 that he might give up drinking alcohol forever. I silently prayed that he would, but he proved unable (or unwilling) to stay away from booze when Easter Sunday arrived. Like Mom, Dad appears to be drinking less, however. I believe both of my parents are concerned now about the death of a number of their friends from liver disease and heart attacks and are becoming more health-conscious.

Looking back, I believe that the biggest problem I had with my mother was my complete discomfort regarding her drinking. She tended to slur her words and be unsteady on her feet. My father held his liquor better, but not always well. He did not lurch or stagger, as Mom did, but he became verbally abusive to me and my brothers. Dad also tended to become more formal, distant and demanding of his children, insisting that we live our lives in an unnaturally confining manner. I tended to shut out my father's words when he spoke to me during the cocktail hour. The habit of not listening to my father eventually became a permanent condition, which continued until he and I went into business together when I was twenty-two.

Neither parent was an ideal role model for me as I was growing up. Still, I tended to feel closer to my father because we were both males. I felt that my mother's drunken behavior was undignified for a woman of her social position. I wanted to be an independent, self-sufficient person who was able to think and act for himself. I denied myself the independence I craved in order to remain at home as a "peacemaker" between my warring parents. I

5

knew they loved me, and I thought my presence would keep them together.

At age eighteen, I joined Al-Anon to see what I could do to resolve my parents' problem concerning their dependence on alcohol and their related fights which occurred when they were drunk. A man in the group interrupted me and said: "You're here for the wrong reason. You can't change your parents' behavior. You should be here to see what you can do in order to live with them as they are, and always will be, unless they decide to change the way they live." I was stunned by the man's comment, but I instantly realized that he was right. I immediately left Al-Anon. I wasn't ready to accept what I had heard.

I paid a terrible price emotionally for my devotion to my parents. I listened to and obeyed their repressive instructions, because I felt that I had to keep my parents from seeking a divorce. Somehow I blamed myself for their problems. Finally, at the age of twenty, I could not take the tension any more. Both my father and my mother would approach me individually and say: "Jeremy, do you know what your father (or mother) did to me today?" I would shout: "I don't care! Work it out between yourselves!" Then I would storm into my bedroom and slam the door shut. My two older brothers had long since moved out of the house. I was left there alone to deal with my parents' problems. I thought I could change or fix them.

At the age of twenty-two, I was scared stiff, but I decided that I had to move out of my parents' home. My efforts had no effect on them. "Let them divorce!' I thought. "They probably should have separated years ago!" I moved to Chicago where my parents started to call me every night. "Leave me alone!" I screamed at my father when he initially tried to force me to continue my role as their "referee" from my new home. The frantic calls from my parents stopped in a matter of weeks. Now we hold very pleasant phone conversations. This rational level of interaction has slowly evolved over a period of two years. I am happy to report that my parents were able to resolve most (if not all) of their differences. However, it was the finality of my action of leaving the homestead which finally caused them to work things out.

It took me two years to complete the process of my moving out of my parents' home, before I finally did so when I was twenty-two. At age twenty, I spent the summer of 1969 with a local widow in Lake Forest. The woman was confined to a wheelchair because of polio which had paralyzed her legs some years before. Mrs. Brompton was a totally self-sufficient person who raised three children alone, despite her inability to walk. She taught bridge and otherwise kept herself exceptionally busy socially.

This lady had numerous friends, including Mr. Simons, who eventually married her. In lieu of paying rent, I assumed the job of keeping the carpets vacuumed and the floor-to-ceiling windows washed in her single story house. Mrs. Brompton cleaned her own bathroom and did her own cooking and laundry. My only other duty was to cut the grass weekly. I stood in awe of my friend because of her total mobility and self-reliance. I initially expected to be caring for a "crippled" woman. Instead, I learned much about self-sufficiency from a remarkably experienced teacher and rather close friend. We never exchanged confidences, but we were amiable with one another. I only left Mrs. Brompton's home because she had announced her engagement to Mr. Simons. There was no reason for me to stay any longer, since Mr. Simons would be doing all of my jobs. I haven't seen or talked with Mrs. Brompton since I moved out of her home. I am sure, however, that she is doing just fine.

I moved from there to the home of Mrs. Welch. She was the Director of Cultural Activities at Midwest College, where I was enrolled. We became close friends. Mrs. Welch struck me as a somewhat nervous person, but totally delightful in her rather frantic and disorganized approach to life. She trusted people, and probably believed that everything would work out somehow if allowed enough time to resolve itself. When I interviewed with Mrs. Welch for the job of houseboy, she gave me a concerned look because I was a male.

"I was really looking for a girl college student," Mrs. Welch said hesitantly.

Something told me to blurt out: "That's awfully closed-minded, don't you think?"

"Yes, it is!" she said in a suddenly determined manner. "You may move in tomorrow!" (Our interview occurred before the term "sexist" came into vogue, which is why I did not think to use the word.) Mrs. Welch was far from being sexist in nature. She read voraciously and often frequented the theatre when she was not hosting numerous dinner parties or going out to parties hosted by her friends. I delighted in preparing the meals, setting the table and cleaning my friend's home. Dinner parties were always held buffet style, so I did not have to serve the food.

Mrs. Welch was a deeply religious Quaker. Her only son adopted that religious persuasion as well. I developed a mild friendship with Mike. He and his fiancée invited me to their wedding at the local Quaker church. It was a unique experience for me, since I had never before seen a service conducted without a minister or priest in attendance. The entire congregation ran the wedding by speaking their good wishes to the bride and groom as they began their lives together. We then signed the guest book, which served as our witness to the marriage. In general, I felt like a part of the Welch family. They treated me as their equal and close friend. I had to move out when Mrs. Welch's daughter, son-in-law and grandchildren came to spend the summer in Lake Forest. They had travelled from their home in Florence, Italy. The children's nurse needed my room, which was located just off the kitchen.

I subsequently moved back to my parents' home for a brief time. The entire preceding year we had barely communicated with each other. I soon dropped out of college and moved to Chicago, where I (oddly enough) decided to join my father's real estate firm. It turned out to be the best decision I had ever made, as our working together allowed us to begin talking to each other again. We grew to love each other a great deal as a result of our sharing the office.

Looking back at those sad years when I was between the ages of ten and thirteen (and still living at home), I can remember dinner parties that my parents hosted, specifically the ones to which I was invited. I have always enjoyed the company of older people, so I was glad to be an invited guest at my parents' dinner parties. Their friends always seemed equally comfortable in my presence, and often complimented me for my maturity at such events. The only regret I had about those parties centered around the times when Mom got drunk and related the story of my birth (in my presence) to the assembled dinner guests. She regaled her friends by describing in vivid detail the way that the doctor and nurses in the delivery room had to strap her down (hand-and-foot) to the delivery table, to keep her from jumping off the surface (when she attempted to physically "double-up" from the intensity of the labor pains). I smiled bashfully every time Mom told this story; but inside I was mortified with embarrassment and humiliation. The story seemed to be a favorite of my mother's, since she often repeated it. Sometimes, the same dinner guests heard it again at different parties. My reaction was always the same. My father never silenced my mother. He was also usually drunk at these affairs and appeared to be uncaring and unaware of my feelings.

I was a sensitive, open child. I listened to the "grown-ups" closely, and believed everything that my elders said and thought. Hearing my mother's story about my birth, I guessed that she really was not happy about having given birth to me. I felt unloved and unwanted. I was also devastated and guilt-ridden, knowing that I had caused Mom so much pain and grief. She is a small woman (five feet, one-half inches tall). I could not bear the thought that I was responsible for making her small frame endure so much suffering. At the age of ten, I told a classmate that I felt my birth was a mistake. My mother overheard my comment. She said nothing at the time, but later that night Mom took me aside and told me how much she and my father truly loved me. I did not believe her statement then. I thought, "How could anyone love someone who gave her so much pain?" Now I have come to realize that both of my parents love me very deeply. Their consistent care and concern for me has proven to me that their love for me is genuine.

From my early childhood until I came out to my parents during Christmas week of 1982, I was not at all close to my mother. We often argued, and although she tried to dominate Allan, Mark and me as children we were not intimidated by her ninety-pound frame. Her regular drunkenness made my mother an easy authority figure to ignore. I am sure that my brothers' and my disregard of our mother's commands frustrated her terribly. In addition to her children's lack of respect, Mom suffered serious physical injuries as a woman in her early twenties. She was in a nearly fatal automobile accident. The bones in my mother's right foot had to be surgically reconstructed, and she had to endure one hundred stitches in her face from the same accident. Today Mom is nearly crippled with arthritis of the right foot. The pain extends up her right leg and into her lower back. She walks with a cane which she has used since 1982. As is my mother's habit, she suffers her physical and mental pain silently. Only recently, in 1984, did my mother allow herself to express her distress. She commented to me over the phone:

"Jeremy, I want to die."

"Why?" I asked.

"The pain from the arthritis," was all she would say. Mom continues to consult doctors, but they seem to be virtually powerless to relieve the arthritic pain which causes her so much suffering. She takes much precsribed medication today which I believe has turned her into a drug addict.

My mother was born in Georgia. Her parents were dominating people who controlled Mom and her sister from birth. As a result of my mother's upbringing, she mostly accepts my father's dictates as the way things must be. Still, my mother has a mind of her own. She is totally charming and gracious around friends. She has a good sense of humor and knows how to make people feel welcome in her home. Today my mother and I are friends, despite her drinking which somewhat distances us emotionally. Although it was Mom's intention to discipline her children as she guided our lives, she was not able to achieve that power over us.

Only our maternal grandmother could do that.

Granny is a strong-willed woman. She is a world traveller who has written a parent's cookbook for proper childhood nutrition and a child's version of the history of Illinois. Granny's daughter, my mother, is not as well-travelled, nor has Mom ever written any books. Granny's credentials made her a more formidable person than our mother, in our young eyes. We three grandsons were somewhat in awe of Granny's accomplishments. Mom suffered in silent jealousy as her children obeyed their grandmother and not their mother. My brothers and I travelled through Europe with Granny, often at her expense. My father does not like to travel, so my mother dutifully stayed home in Chicago with her husband while we children toured the Continent.

Such trips were always fun and educational. We met our grandmother's friends in London, Paris, Zurich, Geneva and Bern, Switzerland. Meeting our grandmother's friends made the trips more fascinating, since those people could explain in detail the history of the cities we visited. They were almost personalized tour guides. Besides, Granny's friends were warm, caring people. I have lost all contact with them, although I retain a lifetime of memories. From age nine until I was twenty-seven, I slowly built a surrogate mother/son relationship with Granny. She was a strict but fair disciplinarian. My grandmother encouraged her grandchildren to be independent in both thought and action.

When I was seventeen, my grandmother announced that I was old enough to think and act for myself. No one had ever asked this of me before, and I was petrified at the thought of assuming responsibility for my own actions. Immediately after her declaration, Granny expected me to select restaurants where we could dine on a weekly basis at her expense. It was my job to make the dinner reservations and to advise Granny where we were eating that evening. She would not allow me to give her advance information about our plans until I picked her up at her apartment.

"Where are we going tonight, Jeremy?" my grandmother always asked with a hint of real anticipation.

11

"To the Cape Cod Room (or Jacques's)," I replied with growing pride.

"A good choice," she would say, with a bow of her head. Granny and I always appreciated *haute cuisine.* We both loved all the same restaurants, so selecting one was not difficult for me. She never disapproved of my selection of restaurants. The ambiance of each dining spot only heightened and reaffirmed the mutual love and respect Granny and I had for each other. My grandmother always insisted on paying the food bill for our dinners together, and she always paid for my hotel room when I visited her three times in Switzerland at ages seventeen, nineteen and twenty-two. I was always grateful for her generosity, though it was usually unspoken. My trip to Bern and the Bellevue Palace Hotel, when I was nineteen, was my surprise present to Granny on her eighty-fifth birthday. She spent every summer there from 1952, when my grandfather died, until 1975, when she was physically unable to make the trip. Granny has not returned to Europe since then.

My plane arrived in time for me to serve my grandmother her birthday breakfast in bed. I intercepted the waiter in the hallway, just as he was about to knock on Granny's door with her tray. I introduced myself to the waiter and advised him that it was my grandmother's birthday. I asked to serve her myself. "Of course, sir," the man said with a broad smile. I took the tray and allowed the waiter to knock on the door."Come in," Granny said cheerily. The waiter opened the door for me. I entered the room, and the waiter closed the door behind me. "Your breakfast, madame," I beamed. Granny was sitting up in bed, wearing her favorite pink bed jacket. She was facing the door as I entered, carrying her tray. "Jeremy!" she stammered as she began to cry.

"Happy birthday, Granny!" I put the tray down on the dresser so I could hug and kiss Granny.

"What a wonderful present you've given me, darling," Granny said, as the tears continued to roll down her cheeks. "I couldn't have asked for more." We talked, hugged and kissed some more until my jet lag set in.

"You need some breakfast, and I need some sleep. I'll go now and see you later."

I stayed in Switzerland a week. It was July 14th when I arrived. A couple of days into my visit, Granny announced:

"Jeremy, here's a map of Switzerland. I want you to select a place to visit. Go there for three days. I'll see you back here, in seventy-two hours." I was flabbergasted. I had never expected my grandmother to suggest that I spend any time by myself. Besides, I wanted to spend the entire week with her, and said so.

"No, dear. Travel is educational. I want you to enjoy yourself, and to learn more about this wonderful country on your own. You can tell me all about your trip when you return." I was exhilarated by Granny's challenge for me to discover new places. I enjoy adventures that take me to places I have never visited and teach me things I have not learned before. I left that day and took the train to Grindelwald, a village nestled in the Alps. The area is famous for its picturesque hiking trails. I must have walked ten miles while I was there. The one night I spent in the town, I met a Belgian couple staying in my hotel. We ate supper together. I told them of my planned trip to Zermatt.

"You'll love it," the wife smiled. "The Matterhorn is lovely." She was wrong; I *adored* the place!

I rode the train to Zermatt. The last half hour of the train ride, I sat transfixed, gaping in awe at the Matterhorn as it loomed ever larger than life in front of me. The July air was clear, cool and crisp. Fresh mountain flowers of every imaginable color and description bloomed everywhere in the lower elevations. Clean white snow covered the mountainside facing me. I praised God for having made such a miraculous place, and for allowing me to witness and enjoy it.

I checked into a hotel and spent hours walking through the village of Zermatt. Only pedestrians and horse-drawn carriages are allowed inside the village limits. I felt totally unrushed and uncrowded as I wandered down the cobblestone streets. I only diverted my eyes from the mountain long enough to glance at the picture-book chalets and the fresh flowers growing in the window boxes of every home. Despite my love for Zermatt, I wanted to return to Bern to regale Granny about my travels and to thank her for urging me to go. Granny's eyes twinkled as I breathlessly related my experiences in the two villages. "I'm glad you went," she said with a warm smile.

The love and respect I have for my grandmother continues even now. She turned ninety-eight on July 14, 1984. She helped me to be the independent person that I am today. I only regret that her health keeps her away from her beloved Switzerland. Granny has hardening of the arteries, which renders her unable to recognize people she once knew. Granny is no longer able to walk, and she talks only in monosyllabic words if at all. Still, I visit her regularly in the nursing home she now calls her home, just in case she ever experiences a glimmer of recognition and once again knows me. We hold hands on occasion, and Granny lets me kiss her on the forehead, which always results in her friendly but confused smile.

Allan is my oldest brother. He is ten years my senior. Because of our age difference, I know very little about my brother when he was a child. I do remember the year when I was three and Allan was thirteen. Our family was living in Key West, Florida, while my father ran the sonar school there. It was his way of helping the U. S. Navy during America's involvement in the Korean War. One day, a hurricane blew into Key West. Such weather is commonplace for the area. It was my first and only experience of coping with such a gigantic storm. I was terrified by the gale-force winds, the pelting rain and the noise of the falling trees. Wind-driven rain was flooding our screened-in front porch. All I could do was to scream and cry at the top of my lungs. Allan picked me up and held me in his arms until the storm passed. I did not stop crying, but I did feel comforted by my oldest brother's presence. The storm ended, and the entire family mopped up the residue of the storm's water on the porch.

Like Mark and me, Allan was educated at private schools. He seemed like a distant figure in my life, because he spent most of his time away at East Coast boarding schools, and at college from the time he was fourteen (and I was four) onward. I only saw my brother when he was home on vacation. Then, Allan seemed very busy with social activities, seeing his numerous male and female friends. The reports I received about Allan came from my nurse or parents. Mary, my nurse, used to belittle Allan about his "wild behavior." She once told me, "You don't want to grow up to be like your brother."

I was amused by the report I received that Allan and some of his friends had thrown wet toilet paper balls onto the roof of the greenhouse one floor below our Chicago apartment. The greenhouse was attached to the single family home next door to our building. Still, I was an obedient child who would not think of daring to emulate my brother's pranks. In time, I became concerned about more of Allan's activities with his friends.

When Allan was sixteen or seventeen, he and some friends were driving our father's car. Allan was at the wheel. His car sideswiped an approaching car on an "S" curve in Lake Forest. No-one was hurt, but there was a long scratch on the left side of my father's car. Dad was not pleased, but it was Mary, my nurse, who told me how "irresponsible" Allan was for having damaged the car.

When Allan was eighteen, he stayed out late at a party with his date of the evening. Rather than driving her home at 3:00 or 4:00 a. m., he brought the girl home to sleep. I understand that one of my parents discovered Allan and his date sleeping, fully dressed, in separate beds in Allan's bedroom. My parents went through the roof about this situation. By now, my brother's reputation as my potential role model was permanently damaged, or so I thought. I felt that I could never trust someone who upset my parents so much.

The final explosion between Allan and our parents occurred when he was twenty. He brought home the bride whom he had married only one hour before. Tricia was twenty-six. Allan introduced Tricia to her new in-laws. I was sent to my room the minute Allan explained why he and Tricia were there. When Allan and Tricia were about to leave, my mother knocked on my bedroom door and entered. She looked visibly shaken. I could tell that she had been crying. "Come downstairs and meet your new sister-in-law," she said. I put down the copy of "Bambi" I had been nervously scanning during the hour I had been relegated to my room. I knew while I was alone in my room that fireworks were probably erupting downstairs in the living room. I was right.

Tricia looked nervous but pleasant as we shook hands. "I'm glad to meet you," she said.

"Me too," I blurted out with great excitement. I was delighted to have a new member in our family. Allan was silent as he stormed angrily out of the room to put on his coat by the front door. Tricia, Mom and I exchanged pleasantries in the front hall until both Allan and Tricia were ready to leave.

"Good luck to you both," I said as my brother and his wife left the house.

Allan stopped halfway through the front door, turned around and solemnly said, "Thank you, Jeremy."

I went into the living room where my father sat slumped in his chair, chain-smoking cigarettes. Tears rolled down his cheeks. "I've lost my son," he whispered. My mother put her arm around Dad's shoulder and hugged him. She worried silently about the son she loved so much, but she chose to join my father in not communicating with Allan.

My parents told me that Allan and Tricia had eloped. That was the first time I had ever heard that word. My father vowed that he would never see or speak to Allan again. I was stunned. The years of negative feedback I had received from my parents and Mary raced through my head. I thought," I can't be close to Allan if Mom and Dad have chosen not to be." My parents did not speak to Allan or Tricia for about a year, until their son, Allan Jr., was born. My nephew was the excuse my parents used to re-establish contact with their oldest son.

Grandfather Simmons was alerted by my father about Allan's elopement. Grandfather took the news very badly. He disinherited Allan in early 1960. Grandfather died in July of 1961, never reinstating Allan in his will, and never speaking to Allan or seeing him again. Grandmother, on the other hand, was a tower of strength. She rallied behind Allan and Tricia, and saw them often. Allan and Tricia were divorced shortly after Allan Jr. was born. I have lost all contact with Tricia, although I hear from my nephew occasionally. He is now twenty-three and is living in Atlanta, Georgia near his mother. I felt enough trust and closeness to Allan Jr. to be able to come out to him in December of 1983.

Allan remarried in 1965. I glowed with excitement and pride when Allan and Patti asked me to be an usher in their wedding. It was then, and until 1978, that I made annual trips to New York where Allan had moved in 1964 and had met and married Patti. Eventually, Patti gave birth to their son, Russell. Patti and I became the best of friends. She once told me in Allan's absence,'"You don't know Allan very well." I replied, "That's true. I'd like to get to know him better, though." Somehow, I never have. Patti and Allan were divorced in 1979. I have only seen her twice since then—once in upstate New York where Patti and Russell live and once in Lake Forest at my parents' home. Our visits were warm and friendly. It was almost as though we had never been apart.

The emotional and physical distance separating Allan and myself has not been a problem for most of my life. We have lived apart quite well. That is not to say our visits have not been friendly when we do meet. They have been. Simply stated, Allan's interests in life have centered around his art business in New York and his family. I have devoted my life to real estate and sorting out my own personal problems. I suspect that Allan did not like the great amount of time I spent trying to build a relationship with our parents and catering to their wishes. I was not the independent, free-thinking and acting person that Allan has always been. I can only guess that Allan grew to lose respect for me because of the conservative, subservient role I admittedly played in tandem with my parents for many years. At that time, I was afraid of Allan and jealous of his fierce independence. Sometimes he got into trouble because of his maverick ways, but he always seemed to "land on his feet" when a crisis arose in his life. I have always admired Allan for his rejection of playing life "safely."

When I was twenty-five, I made an initial, cautious attempt to get closer to Allan. He and Mark had recently purchased a four-unit apartment building in Chicago. I was very upset, hurt and jealous that they had not consulted me or my father about the purchase. I had been in the real estate business for three years and could have helped them find the building they bought. I decided to buy my own building and contacted Allan to see if he wanted to join me as co-owner of a two-apartment building here in Chicago. He said, "Yes," and sent me a check for $7,000, his share of the down payment. After receiving the check I got "cold feet" and did not buy the building. I returned Allan's uncashed check, explaining that I was not buying the property after all. The reason that I decided not to purchase the building was that I could not shake the overpowering fears I had of doing business with my "ne'er-do-well" brother (the term used by my former nurse). Later that year I purchased a different building with my father. His conservative nature and mine complemented each other perfectly. I realize today that I forfeited a wonderful chance to get closer to Allan by withdrawing from our potential partnership but I was not ready mentally to trust or work with my brother.

As this book continues, I hope that my brother and all the people who read my story will see how I have matured and grown into my own free self. I would like nothing better than to develop a lasting close friendship with my brother Allan.

Mark is two years older than I. We were close all during our childhood and into our adult years. Mark has always been the studious member of the family. My earliest memories of him are in the role of a leader for his little brother. We had our occasional disagreements, naturally. Sometimes I felt that Mark was trying to direct my life because he was my "older brother" who was more experienced in the lessons life teaches than I was. Mark had a "B+" average in school, so I figured that he could and should direct my life. I suspect that Mark took his job very seriously. Sometimes I became annoyed when I felt that he was dominating me excessively. I simply felt compelled to irritate Mark to the point that he would hit me. Then I would melodramatically cry my head off while telling Mary the nurse or my mother, "Mark hit me!" Neither my mother nor Mary would let me down. They either spanked or scolded Mark for hurting me. "Revenge is sweet," I thought of these incidents as an older child.

On the whole, however, I have to say that Mark and I got along reasonably well as children. The only problem in my relationship with Mark centered around his superior grades in school. I invariably had the same teachers who had taught Mark two years before me. I was never a good student, and my grade point average steadily declined as I went through grade school. One seventh grade English teacher who had taught both Mark and me had the nerve to scorn my academic shortcomings before the entire class: "You're lazy! That's why you don't do as well as your brother Mark did. Why don't you shape up and be more like your brother?" I was mortified with embarrassment and shame as I slumped mutely at my desk.

I remember all too well the feelings of inferiority I felt whenever I listened to Mark and Dad playing geography games as we drove places in the car. I did not know the answers that Mark rattled off in record time. Dad named all the states in the union. Mark shot back instantly with the names of the respective state capitals. I felt badly, since I knew only a few of the capitals. Another favorite game involved arithmetic. Dad told Mark, "A man was driving his car at 45 miles per hour. How far did the man travel in a half hour?" Mark shot back, "Twenty-two and one-half miles." I was still trying to figure out the question while Mark had already given the correct answer! As this game-playing continued, I soon gave up trying to think of the answers to the questions because I felt that I was not about to do so correctly. I sat wrapped in a gloomy silence, hating Mark for his "superior" intelligence. I also believed that I was "stupid" because I could not compete with my brother.

Dad and Mark also played the game of defining words not commonly used in the English language. Dad gave the word, and

Mark defined it. I listened to this game intently and learned the definition of many words that I had not known previously. My vocabulary expanded as a result of this pastime. Here, too, I could not compete with Mark's knowledge, but I felt consoled because I was learning new words which consequently expanded my education. As a ten-year-old, I chose the favorite word "expectorate"!

By the time I entered the seventh grade, Mark had left home for boarding school near Boston. The psychological damage had been done to me during my years of unsuccessful attempts to compete with Mark. I felt worthless as a student and a person. I decided that the best grade-point average I could achieve was a "C." I went on to schools that Mark had never attended; still, I never worked harder than necessary in order to maintain my "C" average. As my education progressed, I found that I had to work harder and harder to maintain my grades. I finally dropped out of Northwestern University night school with a solid "C" average.

To this day I am still fighting my childhood feelings of mediocrity. Happily, I have made progress in developing a more positive sense of self-esteem. Later in this book I will reveal my accomplishments in business, socializing and an improved state of mental health.

Of my closest relatives, the remaining two adult authority figures in my life were my Grandmother and Grandfather Simmons. I barely knew Grandfather during his lifetime. He died in 1961 when I was twelve years old. I only remember seeing him twice during those twelve years. He was a formidable man, dressed in his ascot and red velvet smoking jacket with a black silk collar. He chain-smoked cigarettes and seemed to snarl at his son, my father. He appeared to be very curt with every one including my grandmother. She seemed formal, reserved and nervous in her conversations with Grandfather. She centered her attentions on him and patiently tried to placate his disgruntled nature.

I do not remember that Grandfather addressed me about anything. As a result of my education in etiquette at home, I never talked to him unless he first spoke to me. Grandfather Simmons died of lung cancer in 1961. Despite the fact that I really did not know him, my parents made me attend his funeral. I sat quietly in my pew at church, wondering why I was there. I felt no sense of loss or remorse that Grandfather had died.

Because of vivid anecdotes that I had heard, I was quite aware of Grandfather's reputation as a prime real estate developer and builder of office and apartment buildings in Chicago. My father gave me a full history of the man I otherwise did not know. I stood in awe of Grandfather because of his accomplishments in the business world. Rumor had it that Grandfather did not get along well with his three children. He certainly ignored me, his grandson, and I suspect that he ignored the rest of his grandchildren. Other stories about Grandfather made him out to be a one-time unfaithful husband to my grandmother. Her reaction was to stand more closely by her husband.

The business world abounded with stories of Grandfather's one-time dishonest dealings with a former business partner. Allegedly, Grandfather bought out his former partner's interests in the company at a lower price than the open market would have allowed. I am not aware of all the pertinent details of the matter, but I understand that the partner had to sell his interests in the company to avoid personal bankruptcy. Grandfather was the only viable client to buy the man's interests in the firm. He did so at the lowest possible price, seemingly taking full advantage of his position of leverage in setting the purchase price.

In general, I understand that my grandfather was both feared and respected by his colleagues in the real estate business. Grandfather knew many influential Chicago businessmen. He had the track record of being able to close some very large, profitable deals. Bankers, presidents of major corporations and private investors flocked to my grandfather's office because they knew that he could make enormous profits for his customers.

About a month after Grandfather died in July 1961, Grandmother invited me to her apartment. We sat in her living room. Grandmother shocked me with the comment: "Jeremy, I don't know you very well. I want to get to know you better. Grandfather wasn't very well during the last few years of his life, so he didn't want company in the house. I want us to become friends." We became very close friends between 1961 and 1973, when Grandmother suffered two broken hips. She then declined mentally until her death in 1980.

Grandmother was a fastidiously formal woman in her dress code and general demeanor. Still, she proved to be a very warm and loving person. Grandmother adopted the policy that she would never telephone any of her grandchildren. She asked us to call her when we wanted to talk with her. Grandmother also never volunteered advice unless people asked for it. Then she gave it, but sparingly.

As a teenager I loved to call Grandmother and make Saturday afternoon luncheon dates with her. Invariably, we ate at the University Club (where my grandfather had been a member). From there we walked to one of the Loop movie houses to catch a matinee. Grandmother lived at an address that required us to walk thirteen blocks to the University Club. It was then an easy walk to one of the movie houses. We walked back home from the movies, another twelve or thirteen blocks. Grandmother was in her early seventies, but she loved the exercise of her daily walks. She broke her left hip in 1972, at the age of eighty-three, when she stumbled over a crack in the sidewalk just outside her apartment building. She was returning home from her daily walk of a mile or two. The doorman at Grandmother's building saw her fall. He picked her up from the pavement and called an ambulance.

The next year, Grandmother was sitting at home reading when she fell out of the chair in which she sat. Grandmother called my father to say that she had "hurt" her right hip. My father called me at my apartment near Grandmother's apartment, asking me to check out her condition. I raced to her apartment and discovered that she had a broken hip. I called an ambulance, and she was taken to the hospital. Ultimately, Grandmother never recovered from the second broken hip. Her mind was failing as a result of complications and side-effects from the first injury. Her mind quickly deteriorated from the added condition of the second broken hip, and seven years later, in 1980, she died of pneumonia.

The years between 1961 and 1973 were a wonderful time for Grandmother Simmons and me. In 1969, I flunked out of college and took my first apartment (a studio unit) across the street and to the west of Grandmother's building. I lived there for six months until I returned to college. During that time, Grandmother and I agreed to meet at her place every Wednesday afternoon after work. I was twenty at the time. Greta, the cook, made fresh lady-fingers and hot tea. She served Grandmother and me in the living room. Greta was a portly Swedish woman in her eighties. She suffered from a form of palsy which caused her hands and head to shake. I always feared that Greta would drop the tray or that items on the tray might crash to the floor. Grandmother sensed my concern and often laid her hand on my knee if she thought that I might jump up from my seat to help Greta place the silver tray and its contents safely on the coffee table. "Greta does just fine," Grandmother once told me gently. I smiled and nodded my agreement.

The teas Grandmother and I shared were unique and marvelous events. Grandmother spent Wednesday mornings at the beauty parlor having her glistening white hair washed and set. When I arrived for tea, she met me in an expensive, brightly-colored cocktail dress and wrist-length white gloves. A lightweight black veil protected her hair, and it extended like gossamer down to her nose. Black patent leather high-heeled shoes completed her attire.

The living room walls were painted a pale blue. Subdued, floor-length gold curtains hung open at the large, bright windows. The room was filled with natural daylight from the east. One could see an expansive view of Lake Michigan to the east and the city skyline to the north and south, nineteen floors below. Teakwood or mahogany tables complemented the French-style chairs and couches that were reproductions of Louis XIV pieces. All the chairs were covered with white slip covers to keep the fabric clean. A glistening black baby grand piano occupied a portion of the living room. On top of it was an overly-crowded cluster of family photographs of every member of the Simmons clan. Grandmother kept the piano tuned for Mark and my father, who were the only two members of the family who could play it.

An ornate rectangular mirror hung on the wall, over the couch where my grandmother always sat when we had tea. I chose a comfortable armchair to my grandmother's right, facing her at a ninety-degree angle. Occasionally I would steal a glance at her straight, stiff back, marvelling at the rigidity she could maintain for hours on end. She had been drilled in finishing school that this was how proper ladies sat. She always sat firmly erect, perched on the edge, but in the middle of the couch. Her feet were planted solidly on the floor in front of her. Her knees and feet remained rigidly together, as her dress just covered the base of her knees. I tended to slouch somewhat in my chair. Grandmother never asked me to adopt her ramrod-backed posture.

Despite our formal surroundings, Grandmother and I engaged in some very free-wheeling and candid conversations. She was a prim and proper woman, accustomed to an outwardly rigid style of controlled body language, but never a prude. One day we discussed heterosexual sex (I was far too closeted to mention gay sex). Grandmother felt that sex was the natural expression of devotion between a man and a woman. She never condoned premarital sex or couples living together before they married. Still, she believed that intercourse was the most sincere form of demonstrative love that two people could show each other.

Another afternoon we discussed profanity. I do not remember the content of our discussion, but I will never forget Grandmother's parting words to me as I left her apartment to go home: "Jeremy, just because the word 'shit' exists doesn't mean we have to use it." I have tried to this day to swear only when it seems appropriate for me to do so. Grandmother only swore twice in my presence. She was not adverse to the use of profanity. She simply thought that it had a proper place and time to be used. I was both shocked and exhilarated by my grandmother's frank-ness. We developed an intensely close companionship and a high degree of mutual respect, love and understanding which remain in my memories of her today.

Grandmother also had a whimsical wit. She once wrote Mark a letter in 1967:

"Christmas cards have begun to arrive. I even received one from my school" (meaning Berlitz). "I shot back my current offering—a wee bit of Venice, and on it I plagiarized without a qualm: 'I migliori Auguri per Natale ed il Nuovo Anno' from an authoritative source, a two year-old Benozzo Gozzoli: Angelo Giardiniere. I had no idea the angels were set to gardening. I'll bet they lie in the shade and brush off the mosquitoes with a wing."

After Grandfather died, Grandmother was lonely and bored. She wanted to master another foreign language. Grandmother already spoke and wrote fluent French. She loved Italy, so she decided to take conversational Italian courses at Berlitz. Grandmother was the oldest student in her class, by thirty years (being seventy-one when she enrolled in her courses). Undaunted by the age difference, Grandmother sailed through her studies and spent the next thirteen years making annual trips to Italy, spending the entire month of May there. While abroad, Grandmother absolutely refused to speak English. She easily made friends with many people—mostly younger, gay Italian men. I had the pleasure of meeting Rudolpho, my grandmother's closest Italian friend. He made the trip to Chicago in 1975 when he heard that his dear friend "Angelina" was no longer physically able to travel to Italy.

Rudolpho was a strikingly handsome man in his early forties. He had jet black hair combed straight back on his head, a slender build, and he wore very expensive designer suits that complemented his physique. Rudolpho was a wealthy country gentleman from Verona who never had to work for a living. He loved to travel at his own expense with my grandmother in her chauffeur-driven car around Italy. They shared hours of delightful conversation about art, literature and architecture. They also reveled in sight-seeing together. Rudolpho knew out-of-the-way places most tourists never knew existed. Grandmother treated

Rudolpho like another son. They were extremely close. The only time Grandmother and Rudolpho spoke English together was in my presence in Chicago since I do not speak Italian. Rudolpho's English was first-rate since he was a graduate of Oxford University. I will miss Grandmother's warmth and charm as long as I live.

During the years when my brothers and I were children, our home was filled with servants. We had a cook, a laundress, a cleaning woman, and—most especially—a nurse. Social tradition and demanding grandparents insisted that my parents must hire what I like to call my family's "domestic army." As an adult, I cynically once told my father, "Appearances of wealth must be maintained for the sake of our family's public image!" The fact is that my grandparents heavily subsidized the large payroll to ensure their children's image as descendants of "old Chicago wealth." I strongly suspect that my parents feared to rebel against the wishes of their families to live the less formal life they preferred. To my parents' credit, they did, in time, dismiss most of the servants, thereby showing their independence.

Given the mass of humanity living under one roof—namely, five family members, a cook, a nurse et al., things had to be run on a tight, sometimes oppressive schedule. Dinner was always at 7:00 or 7:30 p. m. It was understood that Bridgette, the cook, got up early in the morning to make us breakfast. My parents did not want to keep her in the kitchen late at night, cleaning up the dinner dishes, after an already long day there. My mother carefully planned dinner parties with Bridgette's help. It was agreed in advance that such parties would be elegant, but my mother did not want to be unreasonable in her demands upon Bridgette, who had to do much of the hard work.

Often my parents ate alone in the dining room. My two brothers and I were relegated to our bedroom for dinner until we were six years old. By then, my parents believed that we had received sufficient instruction in proper table manners from our nurse and mother to be permitted to dine with the adults on a regular basis. I am not suggesting that we never ate with our parents before we were six. We did so, but only sporadically. Such evenings were grand events. My father dressed in a dark suit. My mother wore her floor-length black velvet evening dress, with pearls and a diamond brooch. Bridgette put on her best black uniform with a starched white apron, and served us our dinner from Sterling silver platters and bowls. The evening was always a candlelit affair with the electric lights turned off.

Part of my dinner instruction involved learning how to remove a modest-sized portion of food from the bowl or platter without making any noise and without spilling anything on the table or floor. Also, I had to thank Bridgette for serving me each meat, vegetable and dessert course. She always smiled and said, "You're welcome." I resented the formality of these meals and felt uneasy about the forced politeness of the event. I have always been a sincere person who does not need to be forced to be gracious.

Bridgette and I were not close, but I liked her gentle, caring nature. She and I spent hours together in the kitchen. I appreciated the fact that she was never too busy while cooking to listen to my childlike conversations about my trips to the zoo or the park with Mary, my nurse. Bridgette's favorite response to my happy, excited reports of the day's events was a genuinely pleased, "That's wond*erful*, Jeremy!" I would then leave the kitchen to allow Bridgette time to prepare the evening meal. Bridgette was a portly, older woman in her mid- to late sixties. She retired when I was eight years old. When she left my family's home, I was sad to see her go.

Our family dinners were highly structured. My brothers and I were not allowed to hold cross-conversations or interrupt our parents when they were speaking. We obeyed the rule that children were forbidden to speak unless we were first addressed by one of our parents. So, the Simmons sons all ate meals in total silence, waiting our chance to participate in the evening's conversation. I recall my parents drinking more heavily during each of the first six years of my life at these dinners. I recall being told I could not leave the table until I had first drunk my glass of wine *and* my glass of milk. I became a shy, quiet child as a result of these meals during which so little was shared. I grew to feel that my opinions were of little or no value. Furthermore, no child could be excused from the table at the end of the meal unless our mother first gave us permission to leave.

We had a dress code as well. No son could appear at the table unless he was wearing a clean white shirt, gray slacks, a jacket, tie and freshly polished shoes. I vividly remember the frantic scramble my brothers and I made before dinner, trying to make sure that we were "presentable" for the evening meal. Naturally, we were expected to bathe (and wash behind our ears) before we got dressed. Our nurse always made a big fuss about our getting ready for dinner in the dining room. I was always excited about the upcoming event, and, at the time, I even enjoyed the flurry of activity. As a teenager, I no longer enjoyed, but rather resented, the preparation for my parents' "inspection" at the dinner table. That anger left me only during analysis when I was twenty.

At the table, when my parents wanted to say something in confidence, they did so in French. My brothers and I did not speak the language at the time, so I felt hurt and resentful about being excluded from the conversation. I was especially upset when I thought about how limited my participation already was in the evening's discussion. I decided to take up French at the earliest possible opportunity in my education. As it turned out, my studies of French began in the third grade. My brothers also learned the language, which caused my father to lament in later years that he and my mother could no longer exchange confidences in French since all three sons could now understand what our parents were saying. I felt a sinister delight in having deprived my parents of this affrontery. Subconsciously, I grew to hate having dinner with my parents when I was younger. I could not open up and say what was on my mind unless I was first addressed. Often, when it was my turn to speak, I had forgotten what I had been thinking. At other times, I simply felt that my comments were unimportant, so I remained silent if Mom or Dad asked my opinions. Happily, those oppressive dinners ended when I was eight years old, when my family moved from Chicago to Lake Forest. There my parents felt that the "country life" of the town was more conducive to a less formal regimen at meals. Still, the mental damage had been done to me in my early years. I was rapidly becoming a repressed, unhappy child.

At the age of thirty-three I brought up the topic of those horrendous dinners to my parents. "I don't remember a thing," my mother commented tersely.

"I do," my father said. "I hated those meals! They were so forced."

"Why did you continue the practice, if you didn't enjoy it?" I asked in amazement.

"Because that's the way my parents raised me," Dad said stoically. "I thought that was the way your mother and I had to raise you boys." I was dumbfounded.

"Children don't have to repeat their parents' mistakes," I volunteered. We dropped the matter at that point. I felt a great distance from my parents emotionally as I was growing up. I relied totally upon our nurse, Mary, for all forms of parenting and affection. On the rare occasions I had a bad dream or could not sleep, I ran to Mary's room, giving my parents' room a wide berth. I looked to Mary for advice and love, which she readily gave. I adored the woman and considered her more my mother than my biological one. Mary and I were inseparable. She was an older Austrian woman who emigrated to America when the Nazis killed her parents and her only brother. The soldiers forced Mary to watch as the balance of her family was slaughtered before her eyes. The story made me feel great compassion and love for my dearest friend. I felt no person should have to endure such tragedy. I probably loved Mary more and showed my feelings more openly to her because of the terrible event she had experienced. I wonder if my parents ever became jealous of my relationship with Mary. I trusted her totally and relied on her wisdom to guide every aspect of my life. Only years later, at the age of twenty, did I realize the terrible price I had paid for giving my entire being and surrendering my freedom of choice to the person I loved so much.

As a three-year-old, I loved to make mud pies after a rainstorm. I rarely did so because I knew that, if I did, I would incur the wrath of my best friend, Mary. She also did not want me to be in the sun for long periods of time. Mary told me calmly, but firmly, how fair my skin was. "You don't want to burn your sensitive skin," Mary would tell me. "No," I said dutifully. Mary also reminded me of how frail I was. She discouraged me from playing with children my own age or with Mark's friends. "You might get hurt. We wouldn't want that to happen, now, would we?" "No, Mary." As a result of my sheltered existence, I had few friends as a child. Since Mary insisted on keeping me indoors and "safe" from the "rough-housing" she thought I would encounter with other children, Mark was almost exclusively my only playmate. I shunned sports whenever I could. It was only in my middle teens that I discovered the joys of swimming and sun bathing. I continue to enjoy these activities today.

At age six I was sent to first grade and on to the rest of my education. My parents did not believe public schools had an adequate curriculum for students, so my brothers and I only attended private schools during our years of study. My nurse's influence on me began to diminish as my school influences increased. I was forced to socialize and play games with my classmates. I made some friends along the way, although I was a very nervous child around my contemporaries. I much preferred the company of adults, with whom I felt on equal footing. I often lectured my classmates about the impropriety of the activities which they pursued (specifically those things of which I knew Mary would disapprove). My classmates either ignored me or belittled me for telling them how to behave. I never used Mary's name as the source of my instructions. I felt that my counsel had inherent merit and could stand on its own qualities of rightness. As a result of my disciplinary nature I had few friends. The few people who liked me already acted in such a way that I did not have to correct their behavior. Basically they were other lonely, docile children. Two of those people, Marty and Paul, remain my closest adult friends. Marty is married with two daughters. He and his family live near Boston, where he attends Massachusetts Institute of Technology as a late-blooming undergraduate student. Paul is a heterosexual bachelor living in Santa Fe, New Mexico, where he pursues a career as a banker. The three of us still keep in touch by telephone or in person. In general, someone I consider to be a friend remains one for life. Only one former lover (I will discuss him in a later chapter) ceased to remain my friend after we parted. I am basically a fanatically loyal person when it comes to supporting the people I like.

As a child, I was often ill. I had the usual childhood diseases of mumps, measles and chicken pox. I also had a serious bout of pneumonia that made me very sick. Furthermore, I suffered the usual number of colds and sore throats. Soon I discovered the ploy of using the many symptoms of legitimate diseases I could choose from to feign imaginary colds and upset stomachs. I pretended to be ill on school days when I was either expected to participate in an athletic event or was having a fight with a classmate. Both my mother and Mary felt the magic indicator of my being truly ill was measurable if I had a fever. I soon learned to elevate the temperature of the thermometer on warm radiators or under warm blankets if the heat was turned off. I did not realize the real reason behind my hatred of sports so much at the time, but I learned the answer at the age of seventeen. I will discuss that resolution of the situation later in this book.

Mary was a fundamentalist Lutheran. She attended services weekly and supplemented her worship with numerous evenings of watching the Reverend Billy Graham on television. I was delighted to join Mary to watch Reverend Graham because I wanted to spend every waking moment with her. I listened intently to Mr. Graham's sermons, absorbing his words like a sponge. I became obsessed with the man's message about people's sinning and going to Hell. I also came to believe that, by definition, all people are born sinners, and are thereby innately evil—not worthy of living on earth. Very quickly, I lost all self-confidence and self-esteem.

Mary and I discussed sin and Hell. She did not ever tell me

that I should not worry about such matters. Instead, she said that if I was a "very good little boy", I, too, could be saved and go to Heaven when I died. I became obsessed with the idea of doing as I was told so that I would be "good" and thereby have a chance of seeing God's mercy when He sent me to Heaven. I fanatically obeyed Mary's instructions to be neat, quiet, obedient, and polite to my elders. My parents reinforced these rules, so I dutifully did as I was told, causing my negative self-image to grow. I felt that my role in life was to obey, and that what I thought and felt did not matter. I was totally controlled by other people.

Mary and Dr. Graham were not the only religious factors in my life. My maternal grandmother was deeply religious. My parents forced Allan, Mark and me to attend Sunday school and church services on a weekly basis, even though they did not join us. Until I was fifteen years old, I routinely attended church services with my brothers.

Sunday school left no lasting impressions on me, either positive or negative. The main psychological and spiritual impact of my years in church occurred during the regular church service, after Sunday school. There I witnessed the ultraconservative structure of the Episcopal morning prayer service. It seemed like every prayer the congregation recited with the minister echoed the theory of how "sinful" and "corrupt" we Christians were. In the content of the sermons, the main message was repeated over and over: mankind possessed the inborn qualities of being weak-willed and sinful, and all these nearly helpless sinners were lucky to be permitted to exist. My guilt grew to excruciating levels, as I believed that I was worse than worthless as a human being. Tears came regularly to my eyes when I prayed to God for Him to forgive my "despicably sinful" self.

Mary was terribly sexually repressed. She never married, and she considered the naked human body something a person should confine to the bathroom while bathing, or something to cover up quickly when changing clothes. I got the distinct impression from Mary that a person's body is somsthing "dirty" and should never be publicly exposed. Until I was twenty, I was very bashful about being seen at the beach or at my parents' country club pool in my bathing suit. I was ashamed of my body and my very slender frame. As the years passed, I could not help but feel appalled by the sight of scantily-clad men and women. Though I was critical of people dressed only in bathing suits, I found that I was visually attracted to the more physically well-developed men around me. I felt guilty about ogling the good-looking men. I did not know what attracted me to them, but I could not divert my eyes from them.

When I was six years old, I asked Mary how people came into the world. Mary contorted her body into the fetal position as she shouted, "Don't ask me about that *filthy* topic!" I was horrified that I had made such a terrible blunder. I did not want to upset Mary by broaching such an unmentionable subject. I had heard stories from my first grade classmates that mothers and fathers somehow got together to make babies. I wanted to check out the facts from a more reliable source. I decided, based upon Mary's strong reaction to my question, that I would never again inquire about this "sordid" matter. I certainly did not want to involve myself with something "dirty" and probably "sinful." I further decided that if my producing children involved physical contact with women I would abstain from all such activity because of Mary's extreme aversion to any physical contact with men.

At age eight, I invited one of my few friends over to spend the night. His name was Tom. He was a quiet boy. I did not know him well, but I was impressed by his stable nature and very good looks. We spent an uneventful evening together before we went to sleep. The next morning, I awoke and went into the bathroom. Tom was sitting naked on the closed toilet seat. He invited me to remove my pajamas and lie face-down across his lap. I did not understand why Tom wanted me to do this, but I was eager to please my friend. He made exaggerated gestures of slapping my rear end. Tom never hurt me. His hand only gently touched my buttocks when it made contact. At the time, only the gestures seemed important. Eventually, Tom suggested that we change positions. I mimicked what Tom had done to me.

I had a strange feeling about my interaction with Tom. I had no idea that what we were doing was remotely sexual, but I tingled with excitement during our activity together. We got dressed, never discussing what we had done. That eventful experimenting was the only time Tom and I spent together outside of school. At age thirteen, I left Lake Forest to begin two years of study at my new East Coast boarding school. I have not seen or talked with Tom since. To this day, I wonder what motivated him to engage me as a partner in our sexual activity. I suspect I will never learn the answer to this question.

When I was nine, my parents decided that Mark and I no longer needed a nurse. Mary was dismissed. I felt crushed that my surrogate mother had been taken away from me. Still, I was willing to get to know my parents better. Soon after Mary left home, I could not wait to ask my mother about the "Facts of Life." I had heard more stories at school that only piqued my curiosity. Mom was somewhat uneasy about discussing the topic, but she did not avoid the conversation as Mary had done. Mom vividly related her impressions about the pain she sometimes felt while having sex with my father. I was shocked and horrified that my father might hurt my mother in bed. I realized that the pain was unintentional, but I immediately reaffirmed my original resolution that I would never have sex with a woman because I would be risking the chance of hurting her. By now, Mom had started relating the story of my birth at dinner parties. I had filed away in my mind Mary's abhorrence of the topic of sex, so I decided such activity was totally inappropriate for me.

By the time I was nine I began to feel unhappy about my parents' escalating drinking problem and their generally oppressive ways. I wanted and needed a more gentle and sober parental figure in my life, so I began to spend more time with Granny.

At age twelve, I attended summer camp in northern Michigan. There I met another twelve-year-old named Andy. We did not know each other very well at all. As in the case of Tom, my eight year-old friend, I found Andy very attractive. One day we found ourselves sitting alone next to the extinguished campfire. We talked about very ordinary things that I cannot remember now. During our conversation, I instinctively laid my head on Andy's lap. He did not shy away. Instead, he gently caressed my face and head. I reacted to Andy's warm and loving touch by placing my arm around his waist. Neither of us directed the other person's actions. Everything was a result of cause-and-effect. A camp counsellor happened to walk by while Andy and I were caressing each other. "Get away from each other!" he yelled. We bolted to our feet. "What you two boys were doing was *wrong*! Don't *ever* let me catch you two together again!" He never did, because Andy and I never saw or spoke to each other again. I returned home from camp, where Marty and Paul filled more of my time with their caring, sensitive friendship. My brother Mark was always available when I needed him, although I was growing to resent his superior intelligence.

For four years I endured many painful dinners as the only son still remaining isolated at home in Lake Forest with my parents, who continued to drink and fight at the table. When I was thirteen, a glimmer of hope for a new beginning and an escape from my deepening mental anguish appeared in my life. It was my enrollment at the new school out East! I was saddened by the thought of leaving Marty and Paul behind, but their positive and happy influences in my life were far outweighed by the more negative influences from the other people and situations affecting me at the time. I understood in advance that I would have to repeat the seventh grade at my new school. I did not care. It was an excuse to leave behind all the misery that I felt while living in Lake Forest. At last, I believed, I had a chance to make a new, happier beginning. Little did I know at the time how drastically my life would change and improve in the years to come!

CHAPTER 2
The Caterpillar

I entered the Gray School for Boys with the eager anticipation of starting a new, happier life. My father flew to Boston with me and drove me to my new school. My first impression of the place was the sight of two hundred boys ranging in age from eight to sixteen, milling around quietly in the outer lobby of the main school building until one of the teachers barked, "Everyone in the study hall for orientation!" We filed into the enormous study hall with its old-fashioned wooden desks that were bolted in neat rows to the wooden floor. A huge moose head hung over the large wooden desk at the front of the room where the study hall master sat. The ceiling in the room was twenty feet high. Large windows occupied most of the wall areas behind me and to my left. The room was bathed in natural daylight, although long, sterile fluorescent light tubes hung ten feet over my head. I sat at my assigned desk as my father stood beside me in the aisle. Tears started to roll down his cheeks as he put his hand on my shoulder. "I have to go now, Jeremy." "Okay, Dad. Thanks for bringing me here." My father immediately left the room.

Mr. Taft, the headmaster, entered the room and walked with great deliberateness to the large desk. As he entered the room the muffled conversation between the students ended abruptly. We jumped to our feet in total silence until Mr. Taft reached the desk and gave us permission to sit down again. I was impressed by the strict discipline of my fellow students and our uniformly well-dressed selves. Each boy was expected to wear a clean white shirt, a necktie, gray slacks and polished shoes. The only time we could remove our ties and jackets was during intramural sports events and related practice sessions and when we slept. We had to call all the teachers "sir" (there were no female teachers), and we had to stand up any time a teacher walked into the room. Third grade boarding students slept in one large, open room. Eighth grade seniors slept two or three boys to a large room. The rest of the student population was confined to tiny wooden cubicles that contained a narrow bed, a dresser, and hooks on one of the walls, on which we could hang our jackets, slacks and shirts. Each dormitory had a teacher who lived in a studio or one-bedroom apartment (reserved for the married men). "Masters," as the teachers were called who were married with one or more children, lived away from the dormitories with their families. Only Mr. and Mrs. Taft lived in Gray House, a large, lovely residence reserved for the headmaster and his family.

My seventh grade year, I lived in a cubicle. The quarters were confining but adequate for me. We had weekly inspections of every living space in the school. Students knew that certain masters dropped a coin on the made-up beds of each student during their inspection of every room. If the coin did not bounce at least six inches after hitting the bed, the stricter masters would tear the bed apart for the student to remake it. The student thereby flunked inspection of his room and would automatically miss the Saturday night movie that all students eagerly anticipated watching. The "untidy" student would have to sit in the study hall with a master while the boy did his homework. Three such visits to the study hall in a row meant that the boy would have to explain his sloppy nature to the headmaster. I never heard of anyone failing to keep his room neat more than once in a while. I was never sent to the study hall. All masters, who inspected the rooms on a rotating basis, always gave me straight "A's" for tidiness. I lived in terror of having my bed torn apart, which meant that the student rumor mill would have labelled me a "slob," if I missed the Saturday night movie.

Other "offenses" that kept boys away from the Saturday night movie were: talking in study hall during regular study hours, throwing "spit balls" of wadded up wet paper at other students, and tossing paper airplanes around the room. I was caught doing the latter by the assistant headmaster. He was monitoring a study hall session one night when I impulsively decided to make a paper airplane and throw it. The plane soared long and high around the room. My initial delight quickly turned to despair when Mr. Thomas grabbed me by my jacket lapel and shook me hard. "I'm stripping you of your movie privileges this week, Simmons!" he snapped. "Yes, sir," I whispered as I lowered my eyes in shame. The boys around me sneaked a glance at me and smiled with impish delight at my "brazen" act of fun and independence.

Students who committed more serious offenses than I were sent directly to the headmaster. Swearing, name calling and fist-fights were punishable by a leather barber strap applied to the boy's behind by the headmaster or his assistant. One boy told a master to go to Hell. The child was in the sixth grade. He received twelve swats of the barber strap (known to the boys as the "flexible flyer"). That was an extreme case. The average number of swats a boy received was three. No child was exempt from possible corporal punishment. I was horrified to learn that a third grader received a swat for saying "damn" in hearing range of a master. I have seen some of my schoolmates since we graduated at different times. We attended class reunions at the school. As adults, they were mentally scarred by their encounters with the "flexible flyer" when they were younger. I was most fortunate in that I never had to feel the effects of the strap. I lived in terror of its presence, however, which caused me to watch every word and deed I performed during the two years I was at school there.

One time I was almost punished by the strap. I instructed another boy to inform a person whom I did not like that I thought he was a jerk. My messenger did his job. The recipient of my message told a master who reported both Kim and me to the assistant headmaster. I was summoned to student court to plead my case. The assistant headmaster was the judge. Before going to court, I approached the boy I had offended with my remarks and apologized. I asked him to tell Mr. Thomas of my apology. Barry did as I asked him to do. I was spared being strapped, but I had to miss the next Saturday night movie. "It takes a real man to apologize for his mistakes," Mr. Thomas told me when he passed the lighter punishment upon me. I was not sincere in my apology to Barry, but I was relieved that I would not have to feel the strap. I ended up writing the lengthy school code of rules *ten times* that Saturday night in Mr. Thomas's presence. Kim, my messenger, received three lashes from the "flexible flyer" for his indiscretion.

During my first year at Gray, I lived next door to a boy named Doug. He was a moody sixteen-year-old who generally kept his distance from the other boys. When he was in the presence of his classmates he spoke with great seriousness and intensity. He also tended to speak very quickly. I was thirteen at the time. Doug's family had lived in South America for a number of years. He was educated there. The American high schools would not transfer his scholastic credits, so when his family returned to the United States, Doug was informed that he would have to enter Gray as a seventh grader. I am sure that he felt great resentment about dropping back so many grades.

One night, Doug entered my cubicle at about midnight. He awakened me. Through my woozy sleepiness I could see that he was sexually aroused as he stood naked in front of me. "I want to show you something," he said as he pulled my covers away from me. He removed my pajama pants and began fondling my genitals. I did not resist Doug's actions. He aroused me and began to masturbate me. While doing so, Doug reached for my right hand and guided it into the act of mutually masturbating him. I had no idea why we were doing this, but I loved the sensations I was experiencing. Doug climaxed which appalled me. I had never before seen sperm, and I did not know what it was. Doug quickly left my room without saying a word. I engaged in my own masturbation until I reached orgasm after Doug left. This was the first time I had made bodily contact with anyone in a year, since I had done so with Andy at camp.

The next night I was very curious to "play" with Doug again. I had no idea what he and I were doing was sexual. It was nearly 11:00 p. m. when I entered Doug's cubicle. He was not asleep. "I thought I might see you tonight," he said. He was already naked, in bed. I undressed. Doug was already sexually aroused. "Lie on your stomach, Jeremy. I want to show you something." I did as I was told. Almost instantly, I wanted to scream from pain. Doug had penetrated me anally with his stiff penis. I had no idea what he was going to do. Doug saw that I was going to scream and thereby awaken the other boys in the dormitory. He quickly stuffed his pillow into my mouth before I could utter a sound. Tears poured down my face from the pain. Doug was a large, muscular boy. I could not move in any direction while he lay on top of me. In time the pain subsided and I began to enjoy the sensation of Doug's phallus inside me. He removed the pillow from my mouth. We eventually reversed positions and repeated our activities. Doug and I learned to engage in extensive foreplay before we penetrated each other. That way, neither of us experienced any pain. Conveniently, Doug and I discovered a jar of Vaseline Petroleum Jelly on the mantel outside our cubicles that the dormitory master, Mr. Edmunds, had placed there. Doug and I used the lubricant on a regular basis. When the jar was getting empty, a new, full jar mysteriously took the place of the old one.

Doug and I visited each other's rooms almost nightly for several months. Then, one day, he contracted a flu bug that was infecting many of the students. Doug was admitted to the school infirmary, where he had to share a room with Carl, an eighth grader. While Doug and Carl shared the room, they were caught in bed together by the school nurse. She walked into their room to awaken them from their scheduled afternoon nap. The woman was horrified by what she saw and immediately called Mr. Taft. Sick or not, both boys were sent home to their families that day. Later in the afternoon, after the boys had left school, Mr. Taft called an emergency meeting of the balance of the student body in the study hall. He explained that Doug and Carl had been expelled for "homosexual sexual activity." This was the first time I had heard the words. I was devastated by Mr. Taft's incensed reaction to what Doug, Carl and I had done. He labelled our activities "sick and disgusting"! During Mr. Taft's thirty-minute diatribe about the "evils" of homosexuality, he threatened to expel "the entire student body, if necessary" to rid the school of such people. I trembled in my seat as Mr. Taft went on to read the following quotation from Leviticus, Chapter 20, Verse 13 of the King James Bible: "If a man also lie with mankind, as he lieth with a woman, both of them have committed an abomination: they shall surely be put to death; their blood shall be upon them." Mr. Taft read other passages from the Bible. Those parts of the scriptures did not have anywhere near the effect on me that the verse from Leviticus did. Mr. Taft spent the entire time he lectured us pounding on the open Bible that lay on the desk below his fist.

At the conclusion of Mr. Taft's speech, I was terribly shaken and upset. All of my childhood religious fears and guilt about sin and Hell flooded my brain. I viewed the event as a sign from God that He was giving me one last chance to change my ways and adopt a heterosexual lifestyle. I felt very badly that Doug and Carl had been caught. Still, I was going to use their tragic experience to benefit my life. I have lost all contact with both people since they were expelled from school. I only hope that they psychologically survived what must have been a terrible ordeal. My reaction to Doug's and Carl's expulsion from school was for me to catapult deeply into the closet for twenty years. I decided that I would never experiment sexually again. I prayed daily to God, asking Him to forgive me for my "perverted" ways.

My prayers and sexual abstinence lasted three days. I began to masturbate daily—sometimes several times per day. I quivered with guilt and remorse about my activities, but I felt that I could not stop myself. Mr. Taft's voice droned away in my head as I heard, time and again, the words from Leviticus. Sometimes the guilt I felt became so intense that I cried after I climaxed. Within a year's time, I no longer heard Mr. Taft's admonitions; but I still felt very "dirty" about masturbating, which, I now realized, I *enjoyed* doing.

During my seventh grade year at Gray, I became a close friend of my dormitory master, Mr. Edmunds. He was a father figure to me. I spent as much time with him as I did with the other boys from the dorm, in his studio apartment. Mr. Edmunds loved classical music, which he listened to on his very expensive AM/

FM stereo system. I like classical music, as well, but I especially loved to watch the red and green sound indicators pulsate horizontally across the indicator screen to the beat of the music. Mr. Edmunds also had the first color television set I had ever seen. There was a large screen on which I could watch cartoons.

Mr. Edmunds was meticulous never to single me out of a crowd of students as his favorite friend, but I knew that he liked me almost as much as I liked him. He saw that I was a sensitive child who needed extra attention. Once, I asked my friend's help to type a chain letter and to make envelopes for the seven people to whom I needed to mail the outgoing letters. Mr. Edmunds was glad to help. While he was busily preoccupied typing at his desk in his apartment, I looked constantly at him, realizing that I loved him. That was the only time we were alone in his apartment together. He asked me to leave his home with the letters as soon as he had finished typing them.

At the age of thirty-four, I learned that Mr. Edmunds was gay. The current headmaster informed me of Mr. Edmunds' sexual orientation during a luncheon visit Mr. Harris paid me in Chicago. I had just come out to Mr. Harris during the same luncheon. He was not the least bit shocked by my news, nor was I surprised to hear that my dear friend was gay. I suspected the truth when I was Mr. Edmunds' student. There was a chemistry between us that was totally nonsexual, but something I have felt only when I am around fellow gays.

My crush on Mr. Edmunds made me enroll in his seventh grade English class. I wanted to please him with better-than-average grades, so it was relatively easy for me to maintain a "B" average in his course. I spent more time with my friend when he conducted the school chorus and church choir. I love to sing, and I wanted to do so for my friend. He never commented about my voice, but his lack of criticism made me believe that my singing was acceptable to him. Mr. Edmunds cast me in the chorus of "H. M. S. Pinafore." Since it was an all boys' school, and since I had a first tenor voice, I played one of the "sisters, cousins and aunts."

Dr. Harmon, my eighth grade French teacher, was Mr.

Edmunds' fellow director of the operetta. Dr. Harmon and I did not get along at all well. He was married and had a son. Mrs. Harmon was a lovely person—shy and quiet—who ran the library. Dr. and Mrs. Harmon's son was a history teacher at Gray. I did not know him very well, since I never took any classes from him. Dr. Harmon used to delight in criticizing me along with a few other select students. We tended to be the quieter, more subservient types of people. I almost did not graduate from Gray because Dr. Harmon wanted to fail me in French during my eighth grade year. Mr. Taft called me into his office about a month before graduation.

"You're not going to graduate from here, Jeremy, if you don't do something about your failing marks in French." I was terrified by Mr. Taft's general presence, but I had the courage to speak up anyway.

"I don't think Dr. Harmon likes me," I said meekly. Mr. Taft looked startled. "Dr. Harmon doesn't even know my first name," I said. "He always calls me 'Simmons.' I'm sure I know enough French to pass the course. I need your help to talk with Dr. Harmon." Then I lost the rest of my courage and remained silent.

"I'll check into this matter, Jeremy," Mr. Taft said with a very solemn look on his face.

The next day, Dr. Harmon called me aside after class. "I like you, Jeremy," he said tersely. "You're just not a very good student." I did not believe my teacher on either count. Dr. Harmon gave me a "D-" for the year, after I had received straight "F's" previous to that. "I must have really excelled these last two weeks," I thought sarcastically when I heard that I would be receiving my diploma after all.

That summer (1964) I attended a Catholic day school near Chicago, where I studied French. I got an "A+" in my studies there. I felt vindicated about Dr. Harmon's personal vendetta against me.

At my luncheon with the current headmaster, whom I mentioned earlier, Mr. Harris confided the suspicions of many administrators and fellow faculty members who wondered about

43

Dr. Harmon's motives for teaching at an all boys' grade school when the man had a Ph. D. in French. His credentials allowed him to teach undergraduate or postgraduate classes in college. Still, the only place he taught was Gray. I suspect that he was a closeted homosexual who took delight in victimizing vulnerable gay and non-gay students who were powerless to fight him. I was lucky. I graduated from Gray and regained my self-confidence. Others did not fight to graduate, and some may not have recovered mentally as I did.

My eighth grade year, I shared a large room with two other boys. I routinely waited for my roommates, Tony and Tim, to fall asleep before I masturbated under the sheets. One night, Tim could not sleep. He heard me masturbating when I thought that the two boys were asleep. Tim got out of his bed and came over to mine. "What are you doing?" he asked. "Jacking off," I said with great embarrassment. Tim quickly pulled the covers off me and sat next to me. Without a word he joined me as we masturbated together. No one said a word after Tim and I both ejaculated. He silently returned to his own bed and went to sleep. I was surprised and pleased by Tim's apparently accepting nature about my sexual activity. Only once during the balance of the time Tim and I roomed together did I ever hear him make the bedsprings creak. It was the unmistakable sound all the school beds made when the boys lay in bed masturbating. I never heard Tony in bed, so I presume that he masturbated elsewhere if he even engaged in such activity at all during his eighth grade year. Neither Tony, Tim nor I ever discussed sex or masturbation during the entire year we roomed together. All students from the youngest in the third grade to the oldest in the eighth grade had to attend Saturday morning anatomy lessons presented by Mr. Taft. The headmaster presented slides from some medical foundation which depicted drawings of the male and female bodies. Other slides showed drawings of male sperm and female eggs and ovaries. Mr. Taft's lectures were usually very boring. Many of the boys thought that they knew more than he did.

Doug, before he and Carl were expelled from school, asked

Mr. Taft to describe the sensations a man felt before ejaculation. It was all I could do to keep from laughing at Mr. Taft's startled initial reaction to Doug's loaded question. The man did not avoid the issue. He meticulously answered Doug in the most clinical way he could. The balance of the student body tittered as Mr. Taft completed his answer. They did not know Doug's malicious intent in asking the question. They were merely titillated by the subject matter and the related answer. I am sure that some of the older boys already knew the answer, as well, of how it feels to masturbate and finally to reach orgasm.

The summer between my seventh and eighth grade years at Gray, I attended the same summer camp in northern Michigan where I had spent the year before. By that time, I had been Doug's regular sex partner until his expulsion from school. I was far too scared to approach any fellow camper sexually. I did not want to be sent home early from camp for gay sexual activities. Instead, I accidentally discovered that I could relieve my need for physical contact with other males by giving the other boys and camp counsellors a "back rub." I had seen professionals give back rubs at Grandmother Simmons's club in Chicago (the University Club). I merely mimicked what I remembered having seen them do. The boys and young men loved the soothing effects of my massages. I loved the physical closeness I could achieve with my associates while they remained unsuspicious of my covert motivations.

At the end of the summer, each camper had to pick a fellow camper's name out of a hat and write a poem about that individual. The poem was to be read by its author on the last night camp was in session. A boy named Brian selected my name. We were not the least bit close, and Brian only knew about my mediocre sports ability and my reputation about giving good back rubs. He incorporated my two characteristics in a delightful poem, most of which I do not remember. Brian gently chided my archery skills, which "missed the mark." He commented how I often came in last in swimming races. Brian concluded the poem with the unforgettable line, "Despite all the critics' barrages,

Jeremy still gives *great* massages!" My initial embarrassment about the litany of my failures in sports was washed away in laughter and pride concerning my superior ability to give massages. I thanked Brian sincerely for having written the poem. He gave it to me, but I have long since misplaced it. However, it is still a favorite memory of my childhood because of its balanced view of me.

At age fifteen I entered high school, vowing that I must remain celibate. I kept that promise, as I stayed deeply in the closet. In order to compensate for my complete abstinence from gay-related sex (except for daily masturbating in private), I assumed a denial attitude about my sexual orientation. I watched my fellow male students mature and blossom sexually as they centered their attentions toward our sister school. During my sophomore through senior years at Bellwood Academy for Boys, I listened to my friends brag about their alleged heterosexual "conquests" of various girls at the Marywood School for Girls. By the time I reached my junior year at Bellwood, I was telling many of the same lies my friends later admitted they were relating. We were a swaggering bunch of proud young men who did not dare let anyone think that one or more of us might be "sissies," let alone still *virgins!* In order to give my stories some possible credibility, I started dating girls at Marywood during my junior year.

I enjoyed the company of some of the girls I dated. I was never attracted sexually to any of them, however. I lived in dread of any girl asking me to have sex with her. That problem did not develop until my senior year at school. One girl asked to have sex with me. She liked me and wanted to show me how much. I shot back, "I didn't think you were that kind of girl!" She fled in guilt-ridden terror. I felt safe, if only for a while.

I spent the rest of my time in class or doing homework, in order to maintain my "C" average. I did have one teacher for freshman year French whom I liked. I had just completed my "A+" summer of studying French at the Catholic school nearby. Mr. Ernest appreciated my knowledge of the language. We used to irritate the balance of the students in the class by conversing with each other in French. For some students, this class was their first exposure to the language. I received an "A" in the class for the year. I had definitive proof (for me) that Dr. Harmon's estimation of my ability to comprehend French was invalid.

During my four years at Bellwood Academy, I became the close friend of a heterosexual fellow named Roy. He was a shy and retiring person, like me, which is why we were probably attracted to each other. Roy was also very nervous about speaking up in class. He was the only son of a couple who lived near the school. Roy lived at home with his parents, while I lived at school during my freshman and senior years. The intervening years, I existed at home with my parents. Roy and I developed a respect and fondness for each other that has lasted to this day. We have exchanged confidences over the years, most of which I have forgotten. We knew that we could trust each other with our secrets.

The summer after my freshman year at Bellwood, I turned sixteen and got my driver's license. "Freedom!" I thought. Roy was somewhat younger than I, so he had to wait nine months to get his license. I spent the summer of 1965 driving to Roy's house to be with my friend. During this time, Roy and I discovered alcohol. I had planned drinking on a regular basis since I was 15. I even thought of getting drunk once in a while. I vowed, however, I would not behave like my alcoholic parents whom I judged so harshly and now firmly hated. I never dreamed that I might have a problem with the substance. I was still highly critical of my parents' heavy drinking, but I thought, "I don't have any problems with booze." I was wrong. One of Roy's friends from grade school lived in the area. His name was Chris. He would join us for beer or wine parties at Roy's house. We closeted ourselves in the basement family room, away from Roy's parents. They knew what we were doing, but Mr. and Mrs. Kennedy never interfered. I guess that they trusted us not to get out of hand with our drinking. Conveniently, Roy's father was an alcoholic. There was an endless supply of booze for Roy, Chris and me because of Mr.

Kennedy's illness. I'm convinced today that I selected Roy as my friend because of the endless supply of alcohol at his house. Still, I denied any personal problem I might have with liquor. Many evenings I drove home intoxicated far beyond the legal limits. It was a miracle, sometimes, that I got home safely. I prided myself on how "well" I held my liquor. I discovered that Mrs. Kennedy was aware of Roy's, Chris's and my drinking when she once told me, "Don't get too drunk tonight. Remember you have to drive home."

Roy and Chris were almost exclusively my only social companions during the school year. During the summer months, my grade school friends Marty and Paul were home on vacation. I tried to divide my time equally between my four friends. Marty, Paul and I drank together as well. Somehow I never got as drunk with them as I did with Roy and Chris.

One night, Chris did not join Roy and me for our Saturday night "drunk." We got onto the topic of homosexuality. Roy commented, "I'm glad I'm not gay." "Me too," I lied. For a person to be gay at Bellwood was unthinkable. We were all a macho bunch of proud boys. Our parents were leaders in the business and social community. Gay men were referred to as "faggots" at Bellwood. The boys considered such people to be weak, ineffective, inferior, and in no way "real men." I certainly did not want my good friend to think of me as a limp-wristed faggot !

Chris, on the other hand, was loud and often vulgar in his language. His personality was in diametrical opposition to the gentler, quieter, good-natured ways of Roy and myself. When Chris joined us for an evening of beer drinking, our conversations usually became loud and profane. Both friends reduced their consumption of alcohol to very modest levels after we finished college. I continued to drink heavily, off and on, until I was thirty-four. Roy eventually married Karen, a wonderful woman I have learned to like a great deal. They now have a son and operate their own print shop in North Carolina.

Chris never married. He pursues a career in real estate sales near Chicago. We are still friends today in our own right. I grew closer to Chris when he toned down his drinking and the volume of his voice. Both men know that I'm gay. I told them when I was thirty-four. Roy's response was the most eloquent of the two men's. He said, "Jeremy, we've been friends for twenty years. Your news today won't change that." I was deeply gratified by my good friend's continued confidence in me. We keep in touch by telephone, and in person when Karen and Roy visit Chris and me in Chicago every year on their vacation.

I used beer as a sedative to dull the pain I felt because I considered myself "trapped" living at home. I hated my parents' drinking and arguing. I did not feel particularly well-liked at school. My grades were dipping below the "C" average that I wanted, and I could not seem to keep them up to that level. My involvement in sports was tearing me up inside. I could not compete athletically, or do nearly as well as my classmates. I was always the last person chosen for teams. In my innermost thoughts, I lusted after certain students (never my close friends). In general, I was not the martinet I had been in grade school. Instead I had become ultrasensitive to the criticism and teasing aimed at me by my contemporaries. I was very nervous about life in general and myself in particular. My instincts led me to believe that life was not worth living when I was sixteen years old. I considered suicide.

My father realized the emotional pain I was suffering. Through a friend, Dad heard about a psychologist in Chicago. "Would you like me to join you at Mr. Aiken's office?" Dad asked. "Yes," I said, relieved to think that I might be able to unburden myself to someone. The influence of my previous religious brainwashing had me believing that I was living in Hell on Earth. I was uncoordinated at sports, unpopular at school, unhappy at home, and generally depressed. I felt that God was letting me down, abandoning me, or possibly punishing me because I had become the worthless person I felt sure that I was. I even doubted the quality of the friendships I had with Roy, Chris, Marty and Paul. My weekly attendance at church made me feel guiltier and more depressed because the prayers I heard seemed to say to me what innate sinners all humans are.

Dad briefly sat in with me at my initial meeting with Mr. Aiken. About ten minutes into the forty-five-minute conversation, Mr. Aiken asked my father to wait for me in the waiting room. Dad left us alone to talk. The first words out of Mr. Aiken's mouth after Dad left the room were, "First of all, Jeremy, I want you to know you're not crazy." I did not think I was crazy, but Mr. Aiken's comment comforted me. "You simply have some misconceptions about life that we are going to work on." For the first time in a long while, I saw a glimmer of hope for myself. I was sixteen when I first visited Mr. Aiken. I thought, "I can trust this man." I spent the balance of the discussion time unburdening myself to my new friend. After the first session with Mr. Aiken, I felt some mental relief. His presence was a much-needed safety valve for me. I had released some of the pressure that stress had caused in me. I was very pleased to know the man. I found him caring, but somewhat distant from me emotionally. I did not care. I decided that I would open up to him anyway.

The next visit I made to Mr. Aiken's office included a discussion with his partner, a psychiatrist named John. He was older than Mr. Aiken, whom I estimated to be in his early forties. John was perhaps fifty. I found John exceedingly compassionate and articulate. Mr. Aiken read the notes he had taken at my first session to John. John talked with me for a while to see what additions I might want to make to the information he had just heard. I had nothing to add. John thought in complete silence for a while, then proceeded to dictate a narrative to Mr. Aiken about my life. Mr. Aiken took down John's words in shorthand.

John began: "I am a very scared little boy named Jeremy. I love everyone very much, but I don't feel loved at all in return." Tears filled my eyes and began to flow down my cheeks as I listened to a perfect description of my feelings. As John dictated his narrative, I could not stop shaking my head in total agreement with the words he was using to describe my feelings. In time, John completed his narrative. He looked at me from time to time while he was speaking. He could see me crying and nodding in agreement with his analysis.

"Jeremy, I don't have to ask you if you agree with what I just said. I can see that you do."

"Yes," I stammered through my tears.

"Good luck to you, son. You'll be okay." Mr. Aiken and I completed the balance of our session in his office.

"I believe in group therapy, Jeremy," Mr. Aiken told me. "Next Wednesday, and every Wednesday that you come here, you'll be part of a group of teenagers your age. I'll warn you that their language gets pretty salty at times. I know you're not used to that. I think you'll be okay, though. Just hang in there." I nodded in dutiful acceptance of my friend's words and left.

No amount of warning could have prepared me for the next six months of group therapy that I endured. My open, sensitive nature was assaulted by approximately fourteen boys and girls who, I felt, must surely have been raised in the streets of Chicago. They were all extremely tough acting, and constantly used really rough language. Many of them had enormous chips on their shoulders. One boy asked me in front of the entire group, "Do you jack off?" I was startled by the frankness and menacing nature of his question.

"No," I lied.

"Everybody jacks off," he said in disbelief.

"Not me," I lied again.

"You must take lots of cold showers, then." The group of kids laughed heartily as I cringed with embarrassment and renewed guilt feelings. I looked frantically at Mr. Aiken for moral support. I wanted him to stop the group from putting me on the spot. He sat silently with a look of anticipation on his face. I quickly felt angry and betrayed that the man I viewed as my trusted friend would not "save me" from my detractors. I had grown up believing that true friends "swept in on white horses to rescue their friends in distress." I decided, at that point, that I would never again allow myself to be vulnerable. I swallowed my pride and instantly adopted the role of antagonist, like the other group members had learned to do. I hated my new image because I became very angry at the world. Still, I noticed that I was becoming a leader rather

51

than the docile follower I had been all of my life before I was sixteen and in therapy. More people flocked around me for advice and friendship. I tried to dominate their lives, which the more docile people allowed me to do. I felt terribly powerful. I still did not like myself very much, but I felt strong and independent.

As my therapy sessions wore on, I noticed that Mr. Aiken was often as antagonistic as the kids in the group were. He routinely belittled me and the other people in the group. I was hurt and felt that I could no longer open up to my therapist or to the other people in the group. I also began to wonder if I might be going crazy. I wanted and needed guidance, so I turned to Granny who was spending another summer in Switzerland. I wrote her the following letter:

"Dear Granny,

I am writing to you today because I need your help. I'm feeling especially depressed because of the way my life is going. Mom is drinking heavily. Dad isn't much better. They fight all the time.

One of my closest friends, Roy, is an alcoholic. Marty is into drugs. He hates his parents and barely speaks to them. I'm crazy, which is why I'm in therapy. Please help me, Granny. I know I can count on you. Where am I going in life? I hate myself. Thanks for being you. I know I can count on you now."

I went on to write a lie to my grandmother: "I'm giving a copy of this letter to Mr. Aiken. Maybe he can help me, too." I never made a copy of the letter, nor did I tell Mr. Aiken or anyone else that I had written it. I then resumed telling the truth:

"I love you very much, Granny. I need your help.

Love,

Jeremy"

Within a matter of days, my grandmother responded:

"My dearest Jeremy,

I'm glad you gave a copy of your letter to Mr. Aiken. I have read and reread your letter with tears in my eyes and great love for you in my heart. You are not crazy. You have problems in your life right now, which I am sure you will work out. I have complete faith in you, my darling. Be strong, and know that I love you very much.

    Affectionately,

    Granny"

    My grandmother's letter gave me strength. It was then that I decided that I had to find a way out of therapy. Relations with my parents and friends were at an all-time low. I was a very angry person who exploded over the slightest thing. I had been with Mr. Aiken for three months, and I felt that he was sicker than I. To my credit, I no longer had any romantic notions about Mr. Aiken, or anyone else, "rescuing" me on a white horse. I realized that I had to feel better on my own.

    After six months of therapy, I asked Mr. Aiken if we could meet privately. I said I felt strong enough to drop out of the group. We met six days later with John. I snowed both men with my seemingly powerful mental attitude. Mr. Aiken praised my speedy improvement as he instantly released me from any further therapy sessions. I politely thanked him for the time we had spent together and left. Riding down in the elevator, I thought, "Thank God I'm out of *that* place!" I went on with my life, projecting a very strong leadership capacity, but feeling scared and basically alone in the world. In time, my belligerent nature diminished. I was relieved that my more sensitive, caring self was returning.

    While I was still sixteen, I received news from Boston that Mr. Taft, my headmaster at Gray, had died. I was ecstatic. The man whose presence I feared most during the two most oppressive years of my life was dead! He made me feel depraved about my sexual activities. Just as I was no longer feeling quite so guilty, I heard that the man had died. "Thank God!" I thought. Impulsively, I purchased an airplane ticket to Boston. I wanted to see the man buried along with the burial of a part of my guilt. Mrs. Taft saw me at the funeral and approached me afterward. She was overcome with emotion at seeing me there.

    "Jeremy, darling! How absolutely wonderful you are to have travelled all the way from Chicago to have attended Martin's funeral." She threw her arms around me and cried.

    "I wanted to be here," I said coldly.

"Martin must have made a very deep impression on you," Mrs. Taft said.

"He did," I responded coldly. Mrs. Taft hugged me harder as even more tears flowed down her face. Obviously she had no idea why I was actually there. I trust that she will never know the real reason.

My residual guilt at the funeral was not resolved in regard to my feelings toward my first sex partner, Doug. From age thirteen until age thirty-one, I blamed Doug for "making me gay." I had hoped that my trip to Boston would eradicate those feelings also, but it did not. I returned to Chicago hoping that my continued dialogue with God at home and at church would resolve my feelings about Doug.

I continued to attend church weekly, but a growing irritation was developing within me about having to endure the highly structured service and its related message of guilt about Original Sin. I did not feel sinful anymore. In addition, I decided that I would not accept the guilt trip that my faith imposed upon me. Over the next year, until I was seventeen, I attended fewer and fewer services at the Episcopal church in Lake Forest. Finally, one Sunday, I walked in the front door of the church, fully expecting to attend the morning prayer service. As I approached the nave of the church, an overwhelming feeling of repugnance overcame me about God and my acceptance of Him. I paused momentarily at the entrance to the narthex and immediately walked on to the rear entrance of the church. I left the building, not to return there for seven years.

At first, I became a staunch atheist, discounting everything I had been taught in Sunday school and at the main service. I figured that there could not be a God because, if there were one, how could He allow me to suffer as much as I had done? When I stopped attending church services on a weekly basis, I felt a great sense of loss. I could not give up my former traditions easily. Even though I believed I was an atheist, I still searched around for a new church to possibly restore my faith. I tried the Presbyterian faith. It was comparable to the Episcopal services I knew so well. The formal, oppressive nature of both religions reminded me of the same condition that existed in my home.

Over a seven-year period, I attended one or more services in houses of worship of the following denominations: Catholic, Jewish, Unitarian, and Quaker. My favorite service was the conservative Jewish service that I attended. I felt swept up by the emotion of the event. My only problem was that I did not understand any of the Hebrew that the rabbi spoke or chanted. Since attending that service, I have learned some Yiddish. I probably could not understand the service, even now, but I appreciate the meaning and philosophy of the language I had superficially begun to learn.

The two Catholic masses I attended made me uncomfortable. The first one was in Latin. I do not speak or understand the language; I never studied it in school. The more modern mass I subsequently attended had a nun playing a guitar. In general, I felt that the structure of Catholicism was too strict and unyielding for my taste. I wanted a religion that gave me the freedom of thought and action I craved.

The Unitarian and Quaker services were too watered-down for my taste. I was especially bothered by the fact that the Quaker wedding I attended had no minister officiating. In time, I decided that there was probably no room for me in any religion and probably no God, so I gave up looking.

By age twenty, I was less certain about my lack of any belief in God. My faith was totally restored, and my lifelong misconceptions eradicated when I was twenty-four. In the next chapter I will discuss this development in my life.

Meanwhile, at age seventeen, I was waging an ongoing battle within myself, attempting to be athletically proficient. Freshman and sophomore years at Bellwood Academy, I played soccer in the fall. All students were expected to participate in the sport of their choice. I chose soccer because I loved to watch the boys in their sexy shorts and tight-fitting shirts. I had tried football in grade school, but I was terrified by the bigger, heavier boys who tended to run over my light, very slender frame. I also noticed that I could not visually follow the course of the football when it was thrown by the quarterback. I tended to stand up in the offensive line. The defensive guard or tackle, opposite me, would knock me to the ground with a hard, jarring thump. Fortunately, I was never physically hurt during these collisions, but my pride suffered terribly as the coach usually kept me on the bench. I did fear getting hurt, and I invariably felt anguish when one of my classmates suffered any injuries.

I set aside my realization that I could not coordinate my eye-hand movements. I rationalized the theory that I was probably ungifted athletically, but I had to participate in sports because the schools I attended forced me to do so. My self-esteem rapidly diminished as my athletic frustrations mounted. I thought, "My poor sports abilities only prove what a worthless person I am." At age seventeen I would discover how wrong my diagnosis was.

Soccer seemed a gentler sport, although that game had its rough moments too. Previously I enjoyed playing halfback or fullback, although I tended to shy away from the onrushing players as they raced toward me. I feared crashing into my friends or tripping over the ball. At least I could follow the course of the ball as it travelled up and down the field. As a member of the soccer team I once again kept the bench warm most of the time, as I had done in my days of playing football. Winter was my favorite time of year athletically. I had a choice of playing basketball, wrestling or swimming. I started my freshman year trying out for the basketball team. That was drudgery for me. I immediately discovered that I had to spend hours privately dribbling the ball and shooting baskets. I needed the practice because, I discovered, I often became separated from the ball when I ran and dribbled at the same time. Developing the skill of shooting baskets required my spending hours standing at the foul line. I experimented to determine the proper distance and arc I needed to put on the ball to toss it through the hoop. All of my meticulous efforts were applied to a very short-lived basketball career. Within a week of my joining the team, the coach saw that I could not coordinate my efforts in a normally-paced scrimmage. I tended to lose the ball, or

I crashed into oncoming players more often than the players with average coordination did. The coach gently told me to try another sport. Even though I could not play basketball, I realized that I loved to watch the boys race up and down the court in their hot-looking, revealing uniforms during competition. I attended every home game at school.

I chose swimming. There I could ogle my teammates in their very tight-fitting, sexy racing trunks. I loved to swim up and down the lanes, although I quickly discovered that I could not race. I tended to crash either head or feet first into the approaching wall of the pool when I turned the corner to return down the pool in a longer race. The coach made me the manager of the team for four years. I won four letter awards from Bellwood for my contribution to the team.

As a hobby, I found that I loved to wrestle with the smaller, weaker boys on the wrestling team. I never formally tried out for the sport. I was afraid to compete and possibly suffer an injury in serious competition. I satisfied myself by enjoying the physical contact with the totally unsuspecting boys, as we rolled around on the wrestling mat in the gynasium.

Springtime allowed me the opportunity to sail in the school lake. We never competed against other schools, but I grew to love the sport. I could semi-recline in the boat as it glided across the calm and peaceful lake. There was a marvelous silence I relished when sailing that made me forget my problems for a while. While on the sailing team, I became friends with a wonderful fellow, Ed. Like me, Ed was shy and retiring. He has remained reserved throughout his entire life, even during the period when I underwent my therapy and related rebellious state. Our friendship has remained intact to this day. Ed lives near Los Angeles now, but we keep in touch by telephone. I see him occasionally when he flies east to visit his parents who live near Chicago.

Ed was my third friend (in addition to Chris and Roy) whose family was not a member of the Chicago Social Register. I was feeling repelled by the ultra-conservative general behavior and thought patterns of the generic upper-middle class. I felt that wealthy people were usually snobbish and closed-minded. Ed and Roy were not that way. Even though Marty and Paul came from rich, elite Lake Forest families, they never acted snobbish or elite. They were more reserved than Ed, Chris and Roy, but I never felt uncomfortable with them. All of us were friends on an equal, nonjudgemental basis. Ed and I shared many happy hours together in high school. He, Roy and Chris were my three closest friends then. Marty and Paul were away at East Coast boarding schools, so I only saw them during vacation times.

Ed's and my sailing days together were fun. He always finished our team's daily races in first place. I always finished second, behind Ed. I did not mind my second-place status. I figured that Ed was a far better student than I was. He graduated second in our class to an absolute genius. Socially, I tended to call the shots when Ed and I were together. I figured that Ed could have the better grades and athletic skills as long as I could dominate our social life together. Ed did not seem to mind this arrangement either. He tended to be shy and lacking in self-confidence outside the classroom and off the playing field. I think that he was somewhat relieved that I took the lead in the social part of our friendship.

Ed and I both hated baseball and track, the other spring sports at school. I remembered as a boy in grade school how I used to duck in terror when the ball was hit or pitched at me. I could not judge the speed or narrowing distance of the ball from me. Freshman year, the track coach demanded that I join the team. He wanted to develop my admittedly long legs. I was woefully out of shape from my general avoidance of athletics, but I had no choice in the matter. Coach Freeling signed me up for the team, despite my protestations. I injured my groin seriously the one and only time I attempted to run the low hurdles. "We won't try the high hurdles," Coach Freeling told me as he took me to the school infirmary to be examined by the nurse.

I tried the long jump after I recovered from the bad bruise I suffered on the low hurdles. My distance covered in the repeated jumps I made was not sufficient to allow me to compete in this event. I was growing to hate myself more because of my lack of prowess in track and field events. Coach Freeling would not let me give up. I finished a solid last in the few hundred yard dashes I attempted. "There's got to be something you can do," Coach Freeling told me. I did not think there was. I tried the mile race. It exhausted me, but I could see some improvement in my athletic abilities there. I always finished near the middle of the pack of runners.

"Let me try the 440 yard and 880 yard races," I volunteered. "Go ahead," Coach Freeling beamed. I was surprised by my comment, but I felt encouraged by my performance in the mile race. I discovered that the "440" was a bit too fast for me. I loved the pace and my performance in the "880." I did not feel rushed or tired. By now, my legs were developing well. They were strong and muscular. I thought I looked sexy. I never won any races in the "880," but I always finished in the top four.

Coach Freeling died of cancer the summer after my freshman year track experience. I was relieved that he would not be around to force me onto the track team for another year. My sophomore year, I signed up for spring sailing where I developed my friendship with Ed. We remained on the team through our senior year.

At age seventeen, I was still tremendously concerned about my generally mediocre athletic abilities. My contemporaries openly criticized my skills, which I accepted as "proof" of my worthless self-image. I was not thinking about this concern when I made a routine appointment for an eye exam with my ophthalmologist. I figured that I had worn glasses since I was thirteen and that it was time to have my eyes checked again.

Dr. Howard had me read the usual eye chart during my visit. She noticed that I was misreading many of the letters or reversing their position next to each other on the chart.

"You're dyslexic, aren't you?" she said.

"What's that?" I asked.

"You're calling b's d's and vice versa. O's look like q's to you." I reread the chart and discovered that the doctor was right. "Do you have problems judging the speed and distance of objects approaching you?" she asked.

"Yes," I said in amazment.

"That's a common problem associated with dyslexia," Dr. Howard said calmly.

Memories of all the years I had spent enduring the barrage of criticism from my fellow students when everyone yelled that they did not want me on their team while sides were chosen returned to me. I told Dr. Howard, "Kids have always told mê, 'Oh, no. Not Jeremy!' when I was the only person left to be selected for a team. I didn't want to be on their team either. I figured I was a klutz, and I didn't want to make their team lose because I was on it." Dr. Howard took me in her arms as I began to cry. She was crying too.

"You're not a klutz, dear. You simply have a visual impairment you can't help. Some people are born with dyslexia. You're one of those people. It's not your fault."

I could see that Dr. Howard was right. It was not my fault I had the impairment. Many pieces of my life instantly fell into place. The average grades I was getting, despite my increased efforts to achieve a better than "C" average, my fear of sports and related inability to excel there, and, most especially, my contemporaries' brutal verbal attacks on me on the game field all related to a disorder I could not help!

An unexplainable calmness came over me as I figured out the source of my miseries. Instantly, I was able to forgive myself for the life-long attempts to accomplish impossible goals I had futilely tried for and failed to achieve. I also instantly forgave my detractors for their ignorance about my condition. I decided that I would not complain or feel bitter about my impairment. Instead, I figured I would learn to work around it. I supposed that my friends and family would not understand the implications of dyslexia, so I kept my condition a secret until I was thirty-three. I wanted to "fit in" socially, which also meant athletically, and that was why I remained silent.

Since my parents did not know about my dyslexia, my father

felt that I should continue my athletic pursuits during the summer I turned eighteen. He bought me a beautiful and expensive set of golf clubs. I had not played the game before, so Dad introduced me to the golf pro at a local club where my family holds a membership. Bob, the pro, was an extraordinarily patient man. He had to be. I felt unable to coordinate my vision with the swing of the club to meet the ball. Bob and I labored together until I had established a reasonably good mechanical approach to the game. I learned not to follow the path of the ball once I hit it. I let Bob tell me how well or how poorly I had hit the ball. After my lessons, Dad and I played a round of eighteen holes. Neither of us was very good at the game, but we enjoyed the time we spent together on the course. We had caddies to carry our bags. I always told my caddy secretly that I could not trace the course of the ball. I never explained why. I simply asked the boy to be my eyes after I hit the ball. None of the caddies ever asked why I could not spot my own ball. They graciously led me down the course so I could complete my game.

In previous years, before I knew that I was dyslexic, my father paid for my tennis lessons and horseback riding instruction. The tennis pro, Art, attempted for a month to teach me the game. My serve was uneven at best. Often my racket fanned the air as the ball fell to the court and bounced. My return shots to Art's serves made me look like a revolving door. I connected with the ball perhaps half of the time. Art suggested that my parents find another sport for me.

Horseback riding was pleasant, but I felt somewhat like a sissy since I was the only boy in my class at school who took up the sport. Courses were taught on an English saddle, without the pommel. Had I been instructed on a Western style saddle, I might have felt less guilty about my equestrian efforts. I thought of the stereotypically macho "Marlboro Man," and his Western style gear and saddle. That kind of horsemanship was acceptable to me.

I do remember one amusing story about my riding lessons, which only lasted one summer. I was always assigned an old nag named Missy. She was fourteen and very gentle. I was also fourteen at the time. My seventeen-year-old female instructor was trying to teach me how to canter. Missy was trained to canter when she heard people say, "And canter!" in a lilting tone of voice. I knew this fact because my instructor got Missy to canter before I could make the horse do it, only using the reins. For several minutes, I tried leveraging the reins as I had been shown by my instructor, to make the horse canter. Missy resolutely continued her steady walk in a circle. Her bit had a rope attached to it. The other end of the rope was held by my instructor, who guided Missy in a circle. My instructor did not hear me whisper in Missy's ear, "Canter, you son-of-a-bitch!" The horse kept walking. I played with the reins some more with no results. Again, I whispered into Missy's ear, "And canter!" She responded perfectly, right on cue. "That's great, Jeremy!" my instructor said innocently. She had not heard my verbal command to Missy. That day, I went home and announced to my parents that horseback riding was for sissies! They immediately arranged my cancellation, and my lessons ceased.

Until I was twenty, I discounted the possibility of people with physical or emotional impairments being valuable people who were capable of making a worthwhile contribution to life. My living with Mrs. Brompton in Lake Forest swept away, forever, my false notion that handicapped people are worthless cripples. Living with Mrs. Brompton, I completely lost the idea that she or any other handicapped person needed pity from anyone. I also saw that I had grown to pity myself because I was dyslexic. The self-pity vanished immediately. My life was not ideal, but I viewed myself as being just as valuable as any other person in this world. I still felt alone as a dyslexic person until I discovered that the late Nelson Rockefeller was far more dyslexic than I. I recalled that he had made it to the Vice Presidency of the United States. Also, Bruce Jenner won great honor for himself and his country in the Olympics despite dyslexia. I discovered that I was not alone with my condition. Accordingly, I no longer felt that I needed to fear it or to harbor any lingering doubts about my self-worth. I do not know how, but—at that same time —I decided that I would create my own successes as an equally viable human being!

My dyslexia resolved many doubts and fears in my life, except one. I was a homosexual who still feared my natural lifestyle because of the generally negative impression shared by the overwhelming majority of heterosexuals who believe that being gay is "wrong." I decided that I would deny what I thought was only a changeable preference in my life. "I'll date girls," I told myself at age eighteen. "They'll make me straight."

I do not especially remember the majority of the girls I dated in high school. We mostly met at dances hosted by Bellwood and Marywood Academies. I tended to go after the less beautiful girls who were generally less popular with the better-looking, and, often, more popular boys. One sophomore coed asked me to slip away with her to her room for sex. I used the comment I cited earlier: "I didn't think you were that kind of girl!" I created the comment on the spot. She fled in embarrassment, which allowed me to feel that I had been "spared" from that "fearful thing" (to me) called sex. I only wanted to socialize with girls at that point. I was not yet emotionally ready to engage in sex.

The summer between my senior year in high school and my freshman year in college, I thought that I had better face my fear of having sex with women. Gwen and I had been seeing each other for about three months. I did not know if she was a virgin, but I felt comfortable enough with her to ask if she wanted to have sex with me. I picked her up at her parents' home and took her to my car. As we got into the car, Gwen asked,

"What do you want to do tonight, Jeremy?"

I swallowed hard. "Gwen, I love you, and I want to express my feelings for you by having sex with you."

"She looked stunned. "Well, I don't love you! I'm going back to the house! Good night, Jeremy." Gwen made a quick exit and left me alone in my car. I went home feeling terribly foolish and hurt that I had opened up to Gwen. We never saw or spoke to each other again. I decided that I would not rush into another attempt to have sex with a girl until I met the right one.

Basically, I felt that women were the only means through

which I could be a socially acceptable adult. At age 18, I believed a heterosexual marriage and children were the cornerstone to a man's success in the business and social world. I did not dislike women. I just did not feel totally comfortable in their presence. Their bodies were both a sexual lure and a sexual threat to me. Society told me that I should be interested in a woman's body. My mind told me I wanted women in my life only as friends. I was in a terrible quandry about what I should do. I decided that if I socialized enough with women, in time one of them would find me sexually attractive. We would have sex, get married and produce a family. In short, I felt that women would make me the heterosexual I so desperately thought I had to be.

While I was struggling with my sexual being in high school, I formed the habit of going to movies by myself when I wanted to think or simply be alone. Often I drove into Chicago to catch a Saturday matinee. One day, I went to the Near North Theater. It is a heterosexual theater that shows popular movies to this day. I noticed that the ticket taker was staring at me. I felt uncomfortable about the man's constant gaze at me, but I diverted my eyes as I handed him my ticket. He tore the ticket in half and pressed my half into my palm, closing both of his hands over mine. I yanked my hand away as I gave him a dirty look. I walked nervously into the theater. I turned my head around to glance at the ticket taker before I entered the auditorium. He was still staring at me with a hurt yet hopeful expression on his face. I walked into the auditorium thinking, "What's wrong with that man? I'm not gay!" I was seventeen at the time.

As I grew older, I became aware of many more men giving me their "cruising" looks. They ranged in age from twenty to sixty. I sometimes looked back at them, but I always felt guilty about doing so until I was twenty-nine. At that age I began my long and scary trip coming out of the closet.

I believed until I was twenty-nine that my future happiness and financial success rested on the premise that I must live life as a heterosexual. I would discover over the years how inaccurate my "being straight guarantees success and happiness" theory was.

CHAPTER 3
The Pupa: Inside the Cocoon

I entered Western University, near San Francisco, in September 1968. I was nineteen years old. I chose this school because it was situated in the liberal state of California and because I was curious about the drug culture, which I wanted to investigate. I had lived a very conservative, sheltered life in Lake Forest, and I wanted to experiment with a more progressive lifestyle. I experienced "culture shock" when I arrived in Stockton. My fellow students made me feel like a "foreign born" midwesterner. They also did not like my admittedly conservative nature. I thought nothing of placing a "support your local police" sticker on my bedroom door. Someone tore down the sign within an hour of my placing it on the door. I felt hurt and angry that someone would touch my property.

Students at the university referred to the police as "pigs." That was the common term of the day for policemen. I had no bad feelings about America's law enforcement officers. I knew better than to withstand the tide of opinion, so I withheld my criticisms of my contemporaries' label of the police. Almost the entire student population came from California. They were a laid back bunch of people whose liberal thoughts were totally foreign to me. I quickly learned to think and act in a more open-minded kind of way, but I still felt uneasy about doing so.

I soon met two freshman men who were regular marijuana smokers. I told them that I wanted to join them in smoking pot. At first they thought that I was an undercover narcotics agent. I wore my hair in a crew cut and wore conservative "preppie" type clothing. I assured Rick and Dave that I was not associted with the police. Reluctantly, they allowed me to smoke with them at a party. I did not feel a thing the first time I smoked "grass." I did not want my newly found friends to know this fact, so I pretended to be high. "Oh, man! This stuff is great," I lied. "I'm really feeling wasted." My friends seemed impressed. Immediately I was accepted into Rick and Dave's circle of friends who routinely smoked marijuana. I became a regular smoker of the drug as well. I also quickly attained a genuine "high" every time I subsequently smoked marijuana.

"You're okay, Jeremy," Rick told me once, shortly after I had joined the group of smokers. "I thought you were a narc when I first met you, but you're not. You're mellow." I beamed at the thought of being accepted by my new group of peers.

I quickly grew to rely upon the effects of marijuana to cushion the ongoing trauma I felt about my not being accepted as an equal with the rest of the students in my life. The more I smoked, the easier it was to parrot the liberal thoughts of the people I wanted to like me. They noticed my more liberal views and warmed up to me somewhat. Despite the increased number of friends I was making, I felt terrible that I was compromising my personal beliefs and actions to be accepted by my peers. I never regretted smoking marijuana. I was only sorry that the drug was now becoming a crutch for me to survive socially with my non-smoking friends. I realized that I was not yet a basically popular person at school, a thought that deeply saddened me. I discovered that a marijuana high made me feel much more relaxed in general about life. I was tired of constantly feeling uptight. I figured, "Why not smoke grass if it will relax me?"

Shortly before the first semester of school ended, a classmate named Bill had a nervous breakdown. The guys in the dorm had been harrassing Bill more than they had done me. Bill was from Hawaii and was treated as a "foreigner" too. He was a very sensitive and vulnerable person who wanted and needed friends. He looked to me to be his friend. I was leery about getting close to him. He was perceived by the leaders of our dorm as an odd sort of person, usually a loner. When he was in the dormitory common room, he generally did not speak with the other students there. "What's the matter, Bill?" some of his detractors would say. "Has the cat got your tongue?" Bill would stand up and leave the room to shouts of "Queer!" or "Faggot!" I never knew whether Bill was gay or straight. I certainly did not feel that his sexual orientation should be questioned because he did not conform to the loud, opinionated majority of the group.

The day Bill left school, one of his major antagonists, a man named Michael, surveyed Bill's vacant room. Bill had left behind some poetry which Michael took to his own room and read. A visibly shaken Michael entered the common room where some of us students were mulling over the fact that Bill had had to leave school so suddenly. Michael interrupted our conversation. "God, I'm sorry I hassled Bill like I did. Here's some of his poetry. It's beautiful! He was a hell of a guy. I feel awful about what I did."

I do not remember the exact content of Bill's poetry,but I do recall that it dealt with picture book descriptions of outdoor scenes, mostly in Hawaii. Bill described very tranquil scenes of flowering trees, bushes and flowers near waterfalls or placid lakes. He had a deep appreciation for nature and the beautiful scenery one could find in Hawaii. Everything about Bill's poetry projected peace, tranquillity and beauty.

I was sorry that I had not allowed myself to know Bill well. He was a rare and gentle person, tormented by his environment. His poetry obviously gave him great inner peace until the determination of his enemies to harrass him was more than he could stand. I instantly feared that I might be the group's next victim, since they knew how vulnerable I was to criticism and teasing. My fears were realized as the group viciously attacked with the idea of "loosening me up."

I spent as much time as I could smoking marijuana with Rick and Dave. I never told them about my fears or about the harrassment I was receiving from the men in my dorm. The drug oriented students and the non drug users were arch rivals on campus. The university did not condone the consumption of alcohol or drugs. Anyone caught in the act of participating in such activities could be instantly expelled from school. To this day, the university is a strict Methodist institution. Cigarette smoking, which I and many other students indulged in, was tolerated.   That practice had only been allowed by the administration a year or two before I entered the school in 1968.

As the term came to a close in January 1969, I felt that I had fewer and fewer friends. My grades were slipping from a "D" average into the "F" range. I felt that I was being taunted mercilessly on the basis of my still conservative ways. I had become far more liberal in my thoughts and actions since I left Lake Forest four months before. The people around me were trying to liberalize me even more. I felt like a tortured chameleon who was not pleasing his enemies fast enough. I certainly was not pleasing myself with the social routine and thought patterns I was assuming outside the drug culture, where I wanted to feel appreciated. I believed that the people who did *not* take drugs were the kind of people I should emulate, rather than my drug oriented friends who were belittled by the majority of the student body.

I kept my association with the drug oriented students a secret from my dormitory associates. Giving that information to my detractors, I thought, could only hurt me socially even more .

I finished my last final exam and returned to the dorm. I packed my bags, anticipating a much-needed week long break from school. I was scheduled to visit a close friend named Ann in San Francisco. While I was packing, I realized how much I hated the school. I hated myself as I felt lonely. I had been toying with the idea of dropping out of school and attending another college where I would feel more comfortable. "Dad would kill me if I left this school," I thought. "I'll kill myself instead."

Impulsively, I opened my bureau drawer and removed a full bottle of aspirin. "These guys are going to kill me if I don't do it first," I thought. I swallowed the entire contents of the bottle. Almost immediately I threw up the pills. "Shit!" I thought. "I can't even kill myself properly!" I went to bed and slept soundly.

The next morning I awoke feeling terribly depressed. "Damn it, I'm still alive," I thought. I caught the Greyhound bus to San Francisco where I arrived more dead than alive at Ann's door. She owned a four-story, expensive townhouse on Russian Hill. She opened the front door with a happy, anticipatory look on her face. That expression immediately changed to one of great concern. She could see that there was something terribly wrong with me. She wasted no time in saying, calmly but firmly, "Jeremy, I want you to take your suitcase upstairs to the fourth floor guest room. Remove your jacket and tie while you're up there and report back to me in the living room on the second floor." "Yes, ma'am," I said meekly. I dragged myself up the narrow staircase to my room. After I removed my jacket and tie, I labored my way down the stairs to the living room. Ann was standing in the doorway of the room with a canister-type vacuum cleaner beside her. She placed the canister and connected vacuum attachment in my hands.

"The stairs are absolutely filthy, Jeremy. I want you to vacuum them immediately. I'll wait for you here in the living room." I gave her a quizzical look but did as she asked. I felt it odd that she had not even said "hello" to me yet.

The minute I began to vacuum the stairs, I found myself crashing the nozzle into the riser of every stair. Tears filled my eyes as I took out my frustrations on each step. Ann was outside my range of view and did not move or speak to me while I was making all that commotion. I finished the four flights of stairs and returned somewhat winded to the living room. Ann stood up from the couch where she had been seated and surveyed the closest stairs.

"They're not quite clean enough yet," she said in a slow, examining kind of way. "Do them again."

"What?" I protested.

Ann raised her right index finger in the direction of the stairs. "Go on, Jeremy, and do as you're told."

"How can I refuse a direct order?" I thought. I returned to the stairs and attacked them again. Now I was angry at Ann. "That bitch!" I thought. "Making me do these fucking stairs again." About halfway through my second trip up the stairs, however, I realized what Ann was doing. A smile crossed my face. I felt a deep love in my heart for her. She was letting me vent my frustrations on her staircase. "What a sweetheart," I thought. My racket instantly ceased. One could hear only the hum of the vacuum's motor during the last half of my trip up the stairs. I finished the stairs and returned to the living room feeling tired but somewhat happier than I had felt before.

"Now we can talk," Ann said in a cheery voice. "How are you, Jeremy?"

"I tried to kill myself last night," I said bluntly. Ann hugged me hard in her arms. We spent the rest of the afternoon talking. During our conversation, Ann called her friends John and Marjorie to join us for dinner. John ran the art gallery Ann owned. I was not privy to the details of the conversation which Ann held on her bedroom telephone. She told me that I could "talk" with her friends, which was why she had invited them over for dinner. Talk we did! John and Marjorie sat in silence, listening to me intently while I related my feelings of fear and sadness about school.

"You need to drop out of that school now," John said. "I used to work for the local paper in that town. The town is the pits. I don't know anything about the university."

"But my father," I interrupted. "He'll kill me if I drop out. Only my brother Allan ever left college before graduating."

"You're not Allan, and you're not your father," John said sternly. I had to agree.

I was petrified, but I decided that evening that my school days at Western University were over. I called my parents the next day to advise them of my decision in the matter. I figured that my life and future happiness were far more important than pleasing my father. I telephoned my parents who were infuriated by the news of my decision. "You can't drop out. I forbid it!" my father roared.

"I've already done so, Dad," I said calmly.

"Now I won't see San Francisco," my mother lamented. My parents and I agreed that I would fly home to Chicago to talk over the situation further. Try as they did, my parents could not change my mind. I returned to San Francisco to pack my bags and ship them home via air freight. I stayed with Ann on my return to the West Coast.

When I returned to campus to pack my belongings, I ran into Michael and Peter who were, by now, my two worst enemies in the dorm.

"Why aren't you still in San Francisco?" Peter asked me. I did not want him to know that his harrassment had been a major factor in my decision to leave the school.

Off the top of my head, I lied, "My mother's had a nervous breakdown. My father's asked me to drop out of school and return home to be with her."

"She's probably sick because of you," Peter said.

"Shut up," Michael snapped. I was surprised and pleased by Michael's reaction to Peter's comment. I could only imagine he was thinking of the way he had abused Bill.

"I've got to run and pack now. The cab is waiting to take me back to the bus station." I returned to Ann's home.

"Before you return to Chicago for good, I want you to visit Berkeley," Ann said. "You might want to attend classes there." I was open to her suggestion, so I made an appointment to meet with the Dean of Admissions. It was 1969, and the Vietnam war protests were in full swing on the Berkeley campus. The quadrangle that separates the Student Union Building from the Admissions Building was filled with chanting students. Armed, helmeted policemen carrying exposed billy clubs ringed the quadrangle on three sides. They stood shoulder to shoulder. I entered the square on the street side, which was the only area not cordoned off by the police. I was petrified by the "armed camp" atmosphere. I walked cautiously through the crowd of milling students toward the Admissions Building. About half-way across the square, I heard a male student shout, "Let's get the pigs!" The wall of policemen facing me charged the student and his friends who were responsible for the comment. The students charged back at the police.

I turned tail and ran through the crowd of students who were now pressing their way against me to enter the fray. I heard the unmistakable crack of a billy club as it hit the skull of a student.

A deep groan of pain accompanied the sound of the club striking. Somehow, I was able to weave my way through the crowd toward the Student Union Building. The victim of the policeman's club raced past me with blood streaming down his face and shoulder length hair. I wanted to throw up when I saw the young man's hair matted in his own blood. He disappeared into the crowd almost as soon as I spotted him. I safely reached the common room of the Student Union Building. I threw myself into an overstuffed chair next to two Black coeds. One of them said, "Child, you look like you've seen a ghost."

"I was in the middle of that," I pointed toward a window from which we could see the melee that was taking place. My hand shook, and my heart was pounding as I gestured.

"Aren't you used to the demonstrations by now?" the other coed asked.

"No. I'm just here from Chicago," I said.

"Man, you don't want to come here if you're not used to the riots," the first coed said. That was the only prompting I needed to decide that Berkeley was not the school for me. When it was safe to leave the building, I returned to Ann's home in San Francisco. I never kept my appointment with the Dean of Admissions.

I told Ann about my involvement in the riots and my discussion with the two coeds. I concluded, "I'm moving back to Lake Forest to attend Midwest College." Ann hugged me. "Good luck to you, dear," she said. I took the midnight flight back to Chicago that night. Years later, I thanked Ann for saving my life. She silently smiled and nodded with gratitude. The dear lady ultimately lost her own life to cancer.

When I returned to Chicago, I was engaged in a cold war with my parents. Basically I did not want to speak to them. I felt that they were completely unsupportive of my attempts to find personal happiness. Midwest College accepted me as a student in March of 1969. The Dean of Students assigned me to share a room with a very nice fellow freshman named Brian. Although we were not close, we enjoyed each other's company very much. Brian, like me, was a conservative person. He was also relaxed about life, which made me feel very comfortable in his presence. His favorite expression, which amused me greatly, was, "Don't let your meat loaf." I always chuckled when Brian left our room using that parting comment.

I quickly discovered that Midwest College was exactly the school I was looking for in terms of a relaxed but politically moderate institution. The student body was active in the Vietnam War peace movement, but the majority did not feel compelled to tear down the campus. It was alleged that a small group of militant Black students burned down the old gymnasium during my freshman year. The rest of the Black students and most of the White students were shocked and outraged by the incident. The president of the college decided to board up the shell of the building and leave it standing as a monument to the undirected anger shown by some students. I believe that the daily sight of the burned out building saved many other students from wreaking any more damage on the campus. The boarded up shell was a grim reminder of the loss of a facility all students needed and used, for a cause—the Vietnam war—that was not at all related to the intended use of the building.

While at Midwest, I made friends with a number of people besides Brian. Larry, like me, was a prep school graduate. He had graduated from a school on Long Island. We spent hours together singing folk songs while Larry played his guitar. He was a sensitive person. He did not have many friends, so he seemed to value my closeness to him. I visited him twice in New York, once at his home on Long Island, and again in New York City when I visited Allan and Patti. Larry and I lost touch with each other after he failed out of college and pursued a full-time career in computer programming near his home.

Jack and Tina were two other friends at school. They were high school sweethearts from the Bronx. The three of us smoked marijuana together with another friend, Tony. The latter also failed out of school and joined the Navy before he would have been drafted into the Army. I have lost contact with Tony, although he keeps in touch with Jack and Tina, who have since gotten married and currently live in Wisconsin.

My last and most important friend was a Black student named Joel. He was openly gay at the age of eighteen. All my friends knew and liked Joel. They were concerned about his obvious gay orientation, which earned him considerable gossip and many biting comments at school. None of us wanted him to suffer such treatment. I was basically scared and envious of his openness. Secretly, I wanted to be as settled emotionally about my sexuality as he was about his. Joel was well aware of the comments made about him. Occasionally, a totally insensitive student would ridicule him publicly about his lifestyle. Joel would go to his room to avoid having a fight with the boorish person.

One night, I could no longer keep away from Joel's room. He knew I was gay, and he wanted to have sex with me. He had never come on directly to me about our having sex together, but merely used his constant body language, which tantalized me tremendously, and ultimately wore down my resistance to the idea of becoming intimate with him. One night, I knocked on Joel's door about midnight. A very sleepy eyed Joel opened the door. "I want to have sex with you," I whispered frantically. Joel perked up. Gently, he took my hand and led me into his room. He could see that I was terribly nervous and guilt ridden about what I wanted to do. He caressed my entire body to get me to relax. I did eventually relax and had a marvelous sexual experience with my friend. Immediately after the experience was over, I became very self-conscious again. "I have to go," I said nervously. Joel kissed me on the cheek and let me hurry to get dressed and leave.

I had sex with Joel for almost two years at Midwest College. I basically felt very guilty about doing so before and after the event; but, during sex, I lost all such feelings while I was in my friend's embrace. His loving, gentle style was therapeutic for me both physically and emotionally. I learned to relax in bed. Joel also taught me how to best stimulate him and myself. We were not close social friends, but—to this day—I consider him the most important sexual partner I have ever had. We lost contact with each other after 1971 when I dropped out of college.

Joel was remarkable in his patience with me. One night, while we were having sex, I told him:

"You know, I'm not actually gay."

"Oh, really?" he said, pulling away from me. He shook my hand very formally as we dressed. He then bid me good night. I instantly understood the irony motivating his behavior and smiled with appreciative embarrassment that he did not tease me about my homophobia.

Joel did irritate me once when he told Jack and Tina that we had engaged in sex together. I did not want to be known as a "whore" (or so I thought). Jack and Tina expressed gentle concern that I might be pursuing a difficult course in life for myself. "Be careful," was their only admonition to me. I was acutely embarrassed at being found out. I told Joel that if we were to continue having sex with each other, he must not tell another living soul about it. I still thought that sex was "dirty," and that gay sex was, perhaps, the "dirtiest" type of all.

Simultaneous with my regular sexual encounters with Joel, I decided to investigate heterosexual intercourse with a coed on campus. Penny seemed the most likely candidate. She had a crush on me. I did not find her especially appealing sexually, but she was available. She admired my "strong, silent" image of manhood. Seemingly, she was emotionally needy. We went to her room and undressed. I had never before seen a woman's bare breasts. Penny was well endowed. I instinctively fondled and kissed her breasts, arousing her; but I never penetrated her because I was not at all aroused. She tried to fondle my genitals, but I pulled away in fear. She did not pursue the matter; instead, I excited her sufficiently for her to reach orgasm without our having intercourse. "How did I do?" I asked sincerely. "You're not supposed to ask that question," Penny said. I could tell that she was satisfied because she lay exhausted and seemingly quite content on the bed. We embraced during the "after-glow."

Shortly after my encounter with Penny, I too failed out of college. I had been partying more than I had been studying. I was embarrassed by my undistinguished scholastic performance and immediately decided to return to Midwest to graduate. I was twenty when I moved to Chicago for the mandatory six month waiting period before I could reapply for admission to the school. I found a job as a bank clerk in the Loop. I hated the job, but I relieved the boredom I felt by having tea with Grandmother Simmons every Wednesday afternoon.

My other grandmother and I spent many evenings together also. It was during that time that we had most of our dinners together. I spent the weekends smoking marijuana with Tina and Jack, who were still at school. At other times, I got together with Joel, who loved my visits as much as I did. The people I saw during that period were basically my only friends. I did see my parents occasionally, as I thought I owed them a visit now and then. They were engaged in open warfare, trying to work out the drinking problem and other problems besetting their marriage. Mark was living in Washington, D.C., where he was working. Allan had long since moved to New York.

While a student at Midwest College, I realized I needed therapy again. I was feeling suicidal again. My life long friend Marty referred me to his therapist, William. I needed to resolve my doubts about the nonsexual aspects of my life. William proved to be just the person I needed for this purpose. He was a warm, gentle person who truly cared about me. I had no trouble discussing my recent attempt at suicide with him. I discovered that my thoughts about death were related to the repressive upbringing I had had as a child with Mary and my parents. William showed me that life is always worth living if one adjusts one's sights to reasonable levels and relaxes about one's environment. I no longer felt the need to kill myself. "I want to live!" I found myself saying. "You can, and you will, Jeremy," William told me. I glowed with joy at this discovery.

Thanks to the presence of William in my life, I have been able to adopt the tenets of our discussions to all facets of my life. I am now totally relaxed about life, while remaining very organized and basically reserved. However, I do not allow my reservations and formality to inhibit me. I simply maintain my dignity and self-pride which gets me through the balance of my life.

During the last meeting I had with William, I brought up the subject of heterosexual intercourse. We had never discussed the subject before. However, I felt comfortable enough with him to broach this scary topic. I told him that I could not get an erection around women. He cringed, at which I forced a relaxed look onto my face.

"Don't worry, William, I can handle it. Besides, you're moving to Connecticut tomorrow. I'll be okay." William looked concerned for me.

He said, "Just remember what we've discussed. Use the information you already have to work out the problem." I could tell that he wanted to stay and discuss the matter, but he had committed himself to moving out of state the next day, and I believed that I could and would work out my difficulties.

In the summer of 1970, at the age of twenty-one, I was readmitted to Midwest College. That was when I first moved into the home of Mrs. Brompton. At about that time, I also met a very special person in my life named Frank. He was twenty-two and was just starting college. He had taken five years to complete high school, after which time he took off three years to work and "find himself." He was a brilliant student. He was also very moody. His red hair and beard seemed to match his fiery temperament. Most people allowed Frank to have his way because it was easier to do so than to argue with him, since he could usually make a cogent argument for his preference. On the rare occasions that he could not get his way, he would sulk for hours about the person or thing he could not control. I was always there to comfort him in such difficult hours. We became extremely close friends as a result of my availability during times when he needed to vent his anger about situations that were not to his liking. In time, I grew to devote my entire being to Frank, something he greatly appreciated. I admired his strong leadership and was in awe of his extreme intelligence. I felt that to endure his occasional outbursts of rage at me or at other people was a small price to pay for having such a good friend. I found myself falling in love with Frank.

Through Frank's presence, I was able to wean myself from my craving for marijuana. He never smoked the stuff and did not want me to smoke it either. I was glad to oblige, since I now realized that I was mentally dependant on the drug as a "crutch" in my life. Besides, Frank liked to drink Scotch. I liked it also. We spent many hours at the local tavern getting drunk together. Frank was my latest drinking buddy since Roy and Chris in high school. I did not realize, however, that only I went home to sober up on Saturday nights. Frank kept right on drinking for a day or two. He was sober again by the next Saturday night when we started the process all over again.

Through Frank, I met his other closest friend, Gary. He was an enigma to me. Gary was nineteen and had already been married and divorced twice. He had the habit of starting businesses, then dropping them when they began to be successful. He seemed bright, but I could not understand this pattern of failure. I also detected him in a number of lies he told Frank and me. I quickly stopped trusting Gary, but since Frank liked him I endured his presence, and, in turn, he endured mine. Gary knew that I had him figured out as a basic failure in life; I could not understand what Frank saw in him.

As the years passed, Gary abandoned one business venture after another and treated his many girlfriends in the same way. But Frank, by contrast, graduated as valedictorian of his class in 1974. He also received a Phi Beta Kappa key on Commencement Day. Gary and I joined Frank's mother, Ellen, at the commencement ceremonies. We were all extremely proud of Frank because of his accomplishments.

Between 1970, when I met Frank, and 1971, when Jack and Tina graduated from Midwest, I basically gave up seeing my latter two friends. They were still smoking marijuana, while I no longer smoked; therefore, our common bond of drugs was gone and our closeness evaporated. I was also seeing less and less of Joel, since I felt a mental gratification from being with Frank which was just as stimulating. In later years, I learned that Frank was also gay. Our relationship, however, was strictly nonsexual. Despite the fact that we did not have sex, I refer to Frank today as my "nonsexual lover" of ten years. We were that close to each other.

I began to suspect that Frank was gay in 1972. He generally shunned women sexually and socially. He seemed overly devoted to his mother, who is, in fact, a wonderful person. During an intense private conversation, I instinctively reached to hug Frank. He backed away, saying, "Just because I love you, Jeremy, doesn't mean I want to go to bed with you." I have never equated a hug between two men with a desire to have sex together. I was somewhat irritated by Frank's prudishness and inconsistent thinking and dropped the matter.

Seven years later, I deliberately tried to seduce Frank. We were spending the night together at his mother's apartment. By then, Frank was a graduate student at Southern Illinois University, working on his doctorate in philosophy. I had agreed to drive with him from Chicago to Carbondale, Illinois to help him move his belongings to school. Frank and I were in the living room about to go to bed in the queen sized hide-a-bed we would share that night. (There were no separate beds in the apartment where we could sleep.) I was delighted about the prospect of sleeping with Frank for the first time since we had known each other. I started to unbutton my shirt, secretly thinking that I would excite Frank sexually with the sight of my body. Frank interrupted me after I had unbuttoned only two buttons. "Jeremy, I'm sure you have a lovely body. Please change into your pajamas in the bathroom." I was furious and embarrassed that he had figured out my ploy. I muttered to myself as I changed clothing in the bathroom. Frank and I might as well have spent the night in separate apartments. I respected his wish to refrain from any physical contact. I kept my body on the right side of the bed while he was practically falling out of the left side in order to keep his body away from mine.

Shortly after that evening, Frank asked me, "Have you ever seen my dick?"

"No," I said with some anticipation.

"Do you want to?"

"Sure!"

"No, Jeremy. Sex would only spoil our friendship." Bewildered, I let the subject drop.

Frank never completed his doctoral studies. He had first attended Brandeis University in August 1974. There he was not the privileged student who got his way as had been the case at Midwest. He dropped out of Brandeis at Thanksgiving break. He was secretly drinking heavily to offset the mental pain he felt about his inability to control his teachers. Frank returned home to work in the private sector for three years. He continued to live with his mother during the entire time he was in Chicago.

Frank's drinking worsened. He lost several jobs by quitting on the spot or being fired for arguing with the boss. His friends became fewer in number since they did not appreciate the fact that he drank all their booze when he visited them. Often he passed out on the host's couch and had to spend the night, much to the irritation of the host. Only Gary and I remained close to him. We were able to deal with his now open alcoholism. In 1977, Frank applied to Southern Illinois University for the doctoral program in philosophy. I once asked him what he would do with a degree in philosophy. "Drive a truck," was his response.

He did not last a year at Southern Illinois University. He tried to commit suicide by swallowing a bottle of aspirin. However, since he called the infirmary after swallowing the pills, the school nurse pumped out his stomach and called Ellen, his mother, to come and pick him up. Instead, I drove down there in her place to help Frank pack and return to Chicago.

"I need a friend, Jeremy," Frank greeted me. I extended my right hand, which he shook warmly. (I knew better than to hug him. He could not have handled the contact.) Frank looked very tired and depressed. It was early afternoon, but I could tell that he had already been drinking. His speech was becoming slurred, and his eyes were bloodshot. We spent the night in Frank's off-campus apartment before driving caravan-style in our respective cars to Chicago the next day. "Are you okay to drive alone?" I asked him before we took off on the eight-hour drive. "Yes," Frank said. We made the trip home safely.

Frank never returned to college or to work. Ellen supported her son at home. She, Gary and I endured Frank's increasing rage as his drinking increased. In January 1979, Frank was admitted to a local Chicago hospital in an alcohol-induced coma. He was in intensive care for five days, then in a private room for five more days. There was no money for private nursing care, so Gary, Ellen and I each took eight-hour shifts sitting with Frank while he endured the delirium tremens. That was the worst time for Frank, his mother and his friends. The nurses had to strap him, hand and foot, to his bed to keep him from jumping out and trying to escape from the hospital. He was enraged at being physically confined to his bed. He tried alternately to cajole Gary, Ellen and me to release him. When we refused, he would yell and swear at us. All three of us had to leave the room in order to recover emotionally when Frank was being especially difficult.

One night, I had the 11:00 P.M. to 7:00 A.M. shift with Frank. He was strapped to his bed, flailing around like a fish out of water. While Frank was tossing and turning on his bed, his hospital gown flew to one side, exposing his genitals. It was not a sexual moment for me, but I was impressed by Frank's well endowed body. I silently covered his body as I wondered why he had kept himself away from me physically.

"Let me out of here!" he screamed.

"No, Frank. Just be quiet and try to relax," I said calmly.

"I want to die," Frank said as he stopped squirming. "Life's not fun anymore. Why don't you, Mom and Gary just let me die?"

"We love you too much to do that," I said tremulously.

Frank screamed, "God damn it, get the fuck out of here! I don't love myself, and I don't want you loving me." I stood quietly by Frank's bed, looking down at the man I loved so much. Tears rolled steadily down my cheeks.

Ten days after Frank entered the hospital, the doctors had to release him because he had physically recovered. Ellen, Gary and I convinced him to enter a detoxification unit at another hospital, shortly after he left the first place. Frank went there to appease us. Within hours of his entering the second hospital, he assaulted one of the male nurses, who fought back. Frank landed on the floor. The police took him to jail. His case of assault was later dismissed by the judge, who could see that Frank was a chronic alcoholic when he appeared in court somewhat intoxicated.

The night Ellen bailed her son out of jail after he had assaulted the male nurse, Frank got very drunk and called me at 2:00 A.M. He awakened me from a deep sleep. "This is Frank. I'm very drunk and very angry. I've just given Mom hell, and now you're going to get it." I would not hang up, but sat up in bed, shaking, while my dearest friend in the world ranted and raved at me for half an hour. I remembered my counselling at Al-Anon as a teenager, and my friends there telling me that there was nothing I could do to help Frank; they said that he had to help himself, while my only job was to "let go" and let Frank succeed or fail on his own. I did not believe them, but Frank's tirade at me was the push I needed to let go. "I've lost my best friend," I thought as Frank continued to holler at me. Finally he ran out of words to shout and hung up to call Gary and berate him also.

I saw Frank only twice in 1979. Both times he had a tall glass of straight Scotch with no ice sitting nearby. He sipped the drink sparingly in the presence of Gary, Ellen and me, but he was persistent in his intake of the alcohol. We said nothing because he had told us in advance to remain silent about the drinking he intended to do in our presence. The atmosphere was very tense, and our visits were short.

On the morning of March 17, 1980, Ellen called me at work to say that Frank had died some time during the night. She had discovered his body on the hide-a-bed with the living room light turned on.

"It must have happened during the night," Ellen said with tears in her voice. "Frank got into the habit of sleeping during the day when I was at work. He awoke and drank during the night while I was asleep. We barely saw each other the last few weeks Frank was alive."

"What a day for a drunk to die," I commented. (It was St. Patrick's Day.)

"Isn't it, though," Ellen said pensively.

In a way, I was relieved that Frank's suffering had come to an end. I had lost the best friend I thought I would ever have, however. Happily, I have made other good friends since Frank died, so his loss from my life has not affected me so badly as it might have. At Frank's funeral, I felt the pain of my great loss, but I secretly thanked God my friend had the problem with booze and not me!

Ellen and I continue to see each other monthly. We talk on the telephone weekly. She now knows of Frank's and my devotion to each other. I have even told Ellen of my belief that her son was probably a homophobic, closeted homosexual. Her response to that statement was a classic! She quoted Shakespeare: "Methinks he doth protest too much." While Frank had vehemently denied his homosexual orientation and belittled his friends Tim and Art, who were openly gay, I found out from Art at Frank's funeral that he, Tim and Frank had engaged in sex together. That fact was confirmed by Tim's former roommate, a man also named Tim. Frank did not relax while having sex with Tim or Art, and could therefore not enjoy himself. He felt guilty about having sex with his friends. They never pushed Frank to have sex with them again because of his negative feelings about the experience.

In the four years since Frank's funeral in 1980 I have not seen Gary. As I stated earlier, Frank was the "glue" that held Gary and me together. Frank's death released Gary and me to go our separate ways.

While I was a college student, beginning at the age of nineteen, I became involved in the debut party social life. My family background provided an instant entree to the homes of some very prominent Chicagoans. Their daughters were the guests of honor at some extremely elaborate and expensive parties. Approximately two hundred of Chicago's most elite teenagers and their parents attended these black tie functions. I grew to know some of my peers and their families.

I could not explain why, at the time, but I felt terribly out of place at these parties. I often sat alone or with other male "wallflowers" on the perimeter of the dance floor. I usually got drunk in order to "loosen up" in the presence of so many people. I also hated the forced socializing of people who barely knew each other. I realized the traditional reason debuts are held is to allow prominent single men to meet and possibly fall in love with equally prominent women. I felt forced into a heterosexual relationship with women. I was simply not ready for such a match, but I attended the parties anyway because I knew that people of my background did so whether or not they wanted to. Besides, I figured that such a social scene might make me more interested in pursuing a heterosexual life style.

I befriended a few heterosexual men, most of whom have found wives among the women they met at the debuts. We lost all contact with each other when I decided, at the age of twenty-two, that I had had enough of such forced socializing.

I was instantly dropped from all debut guest lists when I *typed* my regrets to an invitation. My mother saw me typing the response to the invitation. She said, "Jeremy, darling, if you send your response like that (meaning typed), you'll never be invited to another party as long as you live." I knew Mom was correct, but that is why I took the action.

There is a special *handwritten* format used by participants in high society parties. It is as follows:

Jeremy Simmons
accepts with pleasure the kind invitation of
Mr. & Mrs. John Doe
to attend the debut of their daughter
Steffanie
at 10:00 P.M., Saturday, June 1, 1984
–or–
Jeremy Simmons
regrets he will be unable to accept the kind invitation of
Mr. & Mrs. John Doe
to attend the debut of their daughter
Steffanie
at 10:00 P.M., Saturday, June 1, 1984

84

I simply typed my regrets in the above described format. Happily, I have not been invited to another party since.

The reason that I decided to stop attending such parties is that I became concerned about the amount of alcohol I consumed in order to feel relaxed in the large crowd. My childhood shyness and feelings of worthlessness always came to the fore during these parties. My good friends, who were members of the middle class, were never invited to such functions. I did not believe that they or I were any less valuable people in the world at large, regardless of our family roots and income. I resented the fact that I could not bring a college coed to one such party. I called the hostess, the mother of the debutante, and asked if I could bring Irene.

"What's her last name?" the mother asked.

"Sternlieb," I responded.

"Your friend's Jewish, isn't she?" the woman asked.

"Yes," I said.

"I don't think she would have a very good time at the party," the hostess responded. I did not argue, although I knew that Irene had been barred from attending the party because of her religion. I attended the party without her and had an especially bad time that night knowing that she could not be with me.

The last party I attended occurred one week later. It was the most prestigious Christmastime ball held in Chicago. Over five hundred people gathered for the event, dressed in white tie and tails. There was a line of over one hundred people present to shake the hands of the twelve girls making the debuts. I was twenty-two years old at the time. A young man of eighteen stood directly ahead of me. He reeked of freshly smoked marijuana and sported a gold earring in his pierced left earlobe. I thought, "Who needs this bullshit? Irene and my other friends are better people than this jerk!" I stepped out of line and went directly home.

My mother met me at the front door of our house. "Didn't you have a good time, dear?" she asked. "No," I said as I gloomily went to my room. "I'm never going to attend another debut as long as I live." I declined the very next invitation I received in the typewritten response I described earlier.

"Those people are narrow-minded and phony," I thought. "I'm only going to associate with more genuine, open-minded people from now on."

As I grew older, I continued to boycott all formal parties. I realized, however, that not all upper-class men and women are closed-minded bigots. Today I appreciate the relationships I have with a very select number of warm, sincere, liberal-thinking and acting upper-class people. They are as important to me as the less well-bred or educated individuals I am proud to call my friends. All of us routinely socialize together. None of us is concerned with each other's family ties or influence in the business world. We are merely close friends.

Interestingly enough, one of the men I routinely saw at the debuts years ago now joins me from time to time at the local gay bars. He is as proud of being gay as any self-respecting homosexual can be. We talk about those dreadful days we spent together at the parties neither of us enjoyed.

"They are heterosexual marriage factories," Bruce once remarked. "I couldn't wait to get out of that scene."

"How did you leave it?" I asked.

"I simply turned down enough invitations that the social secretary of the parties got the hint I wasn't interested in attending any more parties."

Reflecting on my life from age nineteen to age twenty-two, I now realize that I was not thinking about myself as a homosexual at the time. I stopped attending debuts because I felt like a stranger in a foreign country. The people at such parties lived a kind of life that was totally alien to me. They thrived on male-female relationships, while I could not have cared less about such pairings. My peers discussed the value of having a great deal of money and of attending the "right college." Neither topic interested me at all. People compared their anticipated careers after graduation from college while I knew that I was going into the distinguished profession of real estate. While some people looked down their noses at me because I did not intend to be a doctor, lawyer or stockbroker, I countered their arguments with the fact that my Grandfather Simmons was one of the major real estate developers in Chicago from 1912 until 1961. Only then did the hardline snobs accept the possibility that real estate could be a distinguished career. I was delighted to leave behind such limited people forever.

CHAPTER 4

The Pupa Matures

In 1971, at the age of twenty-two, I was a readmitted student at Midwest College after having failed out earlier. My grades were at an acceptable "C" average, but I was restless. That summer, I passed my real estate salesman license course. I knew that I wanted to be in the business. I simply did not know where. I was once again living, uncomfortably, with my parents. I approached my father's business partner, Harold Quigley, and requested a job in the commercial leasing and management department of Simmons and Quigley. Mr. Quigley made me the low offer of $50.00 per week salary plus half the commissions I would earn filling vacant office space. I was uneasy about the amount of pay, but I accepted the offer anyway. I notified my startled faculty adviser that I was dropping out of school at the end of Fall term, November 30, 1971. I began my new job the next day, December 1. I was glad to leave Midwest College, where I felt I was wandering aimlessly from major to major. I knew that my future happiness and career hopes lay in real estate. To this day, I do not regret my decision.

My father ran the residential management and sales department. His office was far enough away from my desk that we barely spoke to each other. In a matter of months I was able to rent an apartment in Chicago, which allowed me to move out of my parents' home for good.

During the ten years that Dad and I worked together at Simmons and Quigley, a wonderful thing happened to us: we grew closer to each other than we had ever been before. My father began to treat me like an equal business partner. He regularly sought my advice as a fellow businessman rather than as his son. I was deeply grateful for his confidence in me.

In 1974 one of our residential property managers quit

abruptly. He dramatically dropped the keys of his condominium buildings on my father's desk and stormed out of the office. I have no idea what made Jerry leave so suddenly. All I knew was that my father and Mr. Quigley "plucked" me from the commercial department at that moment and placed me under my father's direction in the condominium management department. I was shell shocked by the sudden turn of events, but, by then, I was cautiously optimistic about working directly with my father. He turned out to be a gentle and supportive boss.

Over the three-year period that my father and I shared an office before working together directly, Dad slowly yet surely extended several "olive branches" in my direction. I saw his honest intentions to become my trusting friend. We slowly developed confidence in each other and friendship for each other, feelings which have lasted to this day. Therefore, joining my father's department was not as traumatic or unpleasant as it might have been earlier, before we made our truce.

The only regrets I felt while working with my father involved the consistently low wages I earned, and the fact that he felt compelled to read every business letter I wrote before I mailed them. I must admit that Dad did work hard to persuade Mr. Quigley to agree to the raises I did receive along the way. Also, I learned my father's style of letter-writing, so that fewer and fewer letters had to be changed before being mailed.

After ten years I felt that my time for being monitored should be over. (Seven of those years were spent working with my father.) I still felt that my $12,000-a-year salary was less than I deserved. Therefore, I looked long and hard for a new job. Finally Bruce, at Keynote Realty, gave me a chance to leave Simmons and Quigley. My starting salary was almost double what I had been earning previously. I felt gratified that Bruce did not give me the all-too-familiar line, "Why do you want to leave your family-owned company?" I often felt like answering that question with, "Because my services are being exploited," but I never actually answered the question. I simply contacted more and more potential employers until I found Bruce. He was impressed that I had lasted ten years at my family-owned firm.

Another issue came to the surface. My homosexuality was taking center stage in my mind. I thought of little else. Suddenly, I felt trapped in a repressively heterosexual environment. I was scared and unwilling to come out to my father. Instead, I thought I had to leave silently to experience and accept my true self. Playing the part of a heterosexual, conservative businessman no longer felt comfortable or honest.

My father took the news of my departure very badly. I suspect that he felt I was betraying him, but I did not care. I felt that I was worth more than the $12,000-a-year salary I had reached, and I also felt that I was no longer a little boy needing supervision even to my paperwork. My father has since forgiven me for leaving the family company. He has sold his interest in Simmons and Quigley to Mr. Quigley, who now owns the successor company alone.

When I was twenty-eight (and at that time still employed at the family company), my thirty-year-old brother Mark got married. His wife Linda is a brilliant and fascinating woman. She and Mark dated for seven years before tying the knot. Linda is a graduate of Yale, where she earned her bachelor's degree. She earned her divinity degree at Harvard. Linda was ordained an Episcopal priest shortly after marrying Mark in 1977. She attended Northwestern University, where she received her master's degree in business administration. Linda is a vice president at the First National Bank of Chicago. She assists at church services at a local Episcopal church on the south side of Chicago on Sundays. Her boss at the church, Father Boyle, has become a close friend of my entire family.

I attended Linda's ordination in 1977. She specifically asked me to be there, and I was curious to witness the event, since I had never seen such a rite performed before. I was still a staunch agnostic at the time. I decided that I would not allow my own doubts about religion to interfere with Linda's important day. Her best friend and mentor from Yale, Father Willis, was also present. He gave a sermon that knocked me off my feet! He talked about the symbols of the Christian religion, i.e. the communion bread and wine, and other aspects of the service which showed Christians' reverence to God and Christ. I had never heard anyone refer to the elements of communion as "symbols." Subconsciously, I had grown to resent the idea (which I thought was cast in concrete) that somehow such items were miraculously transformed into the actual body and blood of Jesus Christ at the time of communion. I was overwhelmed by the idea that there was an alternative logic. Certainly I had not believed that I was actually eating the body of Jesus Christ at communion.

Father Willis went on to state that certain parts of the Bible should not be taken literally. "Hallelujah!" I thought, "There may be room for me back in church and in God's world." The service moved me tremendously. One might say that God's Spirit moved inside me for the first time in many years. I learned from Father Willis that God and Christ were indeed one being. For years I had erroneously thought that Christ was not part of God because of the saying, "God the Father, God the Son and God the Holy Ghost." My confusion in this matter began to clear up as Father Willis described Jesus as the earthly, carnal representative of God. I was ecstatic! I joined Mark and Linda at our new church with Father Boyle.

Father Boyle taught me that the Bible should be interpreted in three ways: factually, historically and allegorically. I had previously heard only: "Every word in the Bible is factual. Believe the words or face eternal damnation!" I also learned that in today's world human beings should use the teachings of the Bible as reference material for modern living. There is much wisdom in the Bible, but the words should be translated into modern terms rather than left in the strict formula which reflected the thoughts and actions of the people two thousand years ago. I became aware that I could live through God and Christ rather than under their thumb as I had originally believed.

In later years, after I came out, I noticed a large number of atheistic homosexuals of both sexes. Many of these people were the products of oppressively conservative Christian and Jewish backgrounds. Unquestionably, the majority of synagogues and churches are anti-gay. It makes sense to me that most people would abandon their church and religious beliefs when faced with such opposition to their being and lifestyle. Happily, I have discovered some liberal heterosexual congregations and exclusively gay churches which exist in many parts of the United States. I warmly suggest to all gays who are not militantly opposed to organized religion that there are houses of worship where you and your sexual orientation are welcome! You will not regret trying them out if you are truly open to the challenge of accepting God on terms shared by you and Him. We are all His children and He loves us all very much. We only need to show Him we care about Him. He will return everyone's love to Him far more than any of us can love Him.

By the age of twenty-nine I had a growing fear that I was being perceived as a homosexual. Early in 1979 I proposed marriage to a woman I did not love. We had been dating for six months. Jean turned me down. I was hurt because I had thought that she could "make me straight," eliminating the ever stronger gay-oriented feelings welling up inside me. After my proposal was refused, I felt somewhat relieved that I would not have to perform sexually with Jean. She had pursued me sexually before I had asked her to marry me. I felt that she was ready to be my wife. After she turned me down, I stopped dating her, but in 1983 I came out to her about my actual sexual orientation. Jean commented, "I knew you were gay. That's why I didn't marry you. I didn't want a homosexual husband." To this day Jean has never married. We no longer see each other. I decided to spend my time with my increasing number of gay friends. I believe that Jean always liked me; I just did not want to torture myself mentally by continuing to associate with a person who could have become someone very special in my life but never did.

I decided that I should spread far and wide the news that I had proposed marriage to Jean and had been rejected. I told everyone I knew. Everyone was supportive; I received comments like, "There are other fish in the sea. Keep trying." I came out of the experience feeling that I had now been firmly established as a heterosexual in the eyes of the world.

While dating Jean in 1979, I had my name placed on a gay mailing list of eight millimeter movies and magazines. I was still petrified by the sight of the naked human body, considering it "dirty." Despite my aversion, I could not resist the idea of looking. I spent one year and approximately $3,000 on overpriced movies and books. I developed an extensive library of materials. Sporadically I felt guilty about the items I was collecting in my apartment; at such times I tore up the magazines and sliced the reels of film into small pieces before throwing them away. "I must be straight," I told myself. "Homosexuality is bad."

By mid-1980 I was accustomed to the magazines and films I had purchased. I wanted to see feature length films at the Cinegay Theater. My first visit there was traumatic! I watched scenes of the coming attractions flash on to the screen before me. I was horrified to see actors larger than life on the screen after the tiny figures on my bedroom wall at home to which I was now used. Somehow, larger-than-life shots were disgusting to me. I left the theater approximately ten minutes after arriving there. My hands and body shook as I drove home thinking, "I must not be gay. Those films were gross!" A week later, however, my curiosity got the better of me and I returned to the Cinegay. This time I sat through the entire double feature and previews of the coming attractions. I thought to myself, as I glanced at the many other men watching the films, "I'm not gay, folks. I'm just here because I'm curious."

I returned to the Cinegay on a weekly basis. My "curiosity" was quickly replaced by the knowledge that I was, in fact, gay. I began to relax about being in the theater and started to take notice of the men around me. They, like me, pursued the following course of action which took each person months to complete: first we sat nervously alone, hoping not to be recognized. We made darting glances around the theater to be sure that no acquaintances were present. Next, we selected a compatible person and sat near him. If that person did not appear nervous about our presence, we would sit in the next chair to his. One of us would discreetly begin rubbing the other person's leg on the side closest to us. If the man did not draw away, the hand closest to his leg would gently begin to massage his thigh. Sometimes the recipient of the massage would respond in kind. From there, one of us would unzip the pants of the other person and expose his penis. Masturbation of the individual ensued until the other person ejaculated. (Some of the bolder couples engaged in oral sex.)

At that point, one of two things occurred. Either the participants moved to distant seats to continue watching the movie or meet another partner, or the couple would go upstairs for more intimate sex. The most experienced men avoided all of the above mentioned foreplay and went directly upstairs for immediate sex. They paid their price of admission and went right upstairs to the cruising area without ever watching the movie. I liked to see the films I had paid to watch, but I also enjoyed the time I spent upstairs. There, a number of men walked narrow corridors that opened onto dozens of separate cubicles for sex. Total strangers met and disappeared into rooms.

These rooms were designed in several ways. There were solid plywood cubicles for private sex. Other stalls had clear plastic walls so that neighbors could watch each other while engaging in intercourse. Yet other rooms accommodated only one person; these rooms had "glory holes" (openings in the walls) of two different sizes. The smaller opening allowed a man to place his penis through the hole for other men to engage in oral sex; the larger holes allowed a man to position his rear end to the hole for anal sex with a willing participant on the other side of the wall. The lure of the glory holes was that people who were unconfortable about their looks could use them, if they desired, to engage in anonymous, unseen sex. Only the exposed part of the body was visible through the hole; the rest of the wall was solid plywood.

Still other areas included an open "orgy area" behind a fence of chicken wire. There groups of men could engage in group sex for any interested person to watch or participate. Finally, there was the "torture chamber" for sadomasochistic sex. A "sling" hung suspended from the ceiling. In effect, the sling was a modified hammock on which a man reclined face up. His back was supported by the sling while his ankles and wrists were cuffed at a 45-degree angle to the rest of his body. The sling was angled such that the man's rectum was slightly higher than his shoulders.

The partner to the man in the sling would stand near the reclining person's rectum. The standing man would lubricate his entire hand up to his wrist. Slowly and carefully he would introduce his hand up the recipient's anus, avoiding any damage to the colon. This act is called "fisting." I never participated in such an act, but have been told that it is often terribly painful. I also believe that it can be dangerous if the colon or rectum walls are cut by long fingernails. Only a select few members of the gay community find this form of intercourse appealing.

I tended to confine my sexual activities to the more traditional oral and anal forms of sex in solid-walled cubicles. I wanted to see the entire body of my partner and feel his skin against mine as we made love in private.

Once, I trusted one of my partners enough to bring him home with me for more personalized sex. He was a college student named Ky, a very pleasant young man from Burma. He was just coming out of the closet and felt nervous about being at the Cinegay. I had been a customer of the theater for more than a year. I could see I could trust him, and, therefore, had no worries about bringing him home for the afternoon.

We were in the middle of having sex when my telephone rang; I had forgotten to unplug the phone before getting into bed. The caller was an elderly real estate customer who often became lonely and called me to chat at such times.

"I can't talk now," I told my friend, who was ninety-two years old and rather deaf, necessitating that I yell over the phone. Ky looked concerned about my excessive volume as he lay in bed next to me. My client loved to tease me, and I loved to return the teasing, but at that point the situation was not conducive to such exchanges.

"What's so damned important that you can't talk?" my client asked tauntingly. I grew nervous.

"If you must know, I'm having sex!" I bellowed. Ky looked even more nervous.

"What time is it?" my client asked. I looked at the clock radio near my bed.

"It's 6:00 P.M.," I shouted.

"Jesus Christ! Who the hell has sex at 6:00 in the afternoon?" my friend asked, now openly teasing me.

"I do!" I shouted with a proud laugh.

"Is she pretty?" my client asked with a pixie-like curiosity. I paused and thought to myself, "I can't tell him I'm having sex with a man."

I bellowed, "She's gorgeous." Ky rolled his eyes as he got to his feet and began to dress. His face was purple with embarrassment. I motioned him to lie down again, but he would not obey me.

"Jesus Christ!" bellowed my client. "Call me when you're finished." We hung up. I was able to explain to Ky the reason for my loud tone of voice while on the phone. He nervously accepted my apologies for making him feel uncomfortable, undressed again, and we completed our sex together. Needless to say, I unplugged the telephone for the balance of his visit with me.

For about a month after my telephone conversation with my client, he restricted his calls to me at my office. Whenever he called me there, he would jokingly start our conversations with, "Mr. Simmons. Are you…uh…busy?" I would always laugh and say, "No." I met my customer at Keynote Realty. We have lost contact with each other since I left that firm.

The ticket taker at the Cinegay learned to recognize my face, since I frequented the place seven nights a week. "It must be a good double feature," he said with a smile. I suspect that he figured that I was a hustler, since I thought only such people visited the Cinegay so often. "It's the best set of movies in town," I said with a laugh. The man took my money as he let me into the theater again.

In late 1982 I ran across a sadomasochist whom I picked up as one of my nonpaying tricks of the evening. When we got undressed in the cubicle, the man began to hit me. "Are you crazy?" I asked as I fended off his attacks. "I love you," he said. "This is how I show my love." He then reached for my throat and attempted to strangle me. I gave a karate chop to his Adam's apple, grabbed my clothes which were lying in a heap on the bench beside me, opened the cubicle door, and raced stark naked for the nearest open cubicle to get dressed and go home. As I fled, I heard the excited voice of a man standing nearby: "Go, girl, go!" This comment amused me greatly and allowed me to relax somewhat as I dressed and went home.

I stayed away from the Cinegay for a whole week, which, for me, was a very long time in those days. When I did return, I sat next to an older man in the back row of seats in the auditorium. We embraced passionately. As we did so, I felt him reaching for my back pocket where I kept my wallet. I repeatedly brushed his hand away, thinking, "Oh no. Not again." The man got my wallet before I could move away from him.

"All right," I said calmly, "give it back."

"Give what back?" he said.

"You know. My wallet."

"I don't have your wallet," he pleaded.

"Yes you do. Now give it back."

"Maybe it fell on the floor," he suggested.

Since the fellow was much larger and stronger than I was, I decided to "play dumb" and go along with his charade. I groped around on the filthy floor, pretending to look for my wallet. After about thirty seconds, I announced, "I'm going to find the manager. He's got a flashlight, and he can help me find my wallet." The man pretended to reach under his seat. He sat up quickly, holding my wallet in his hand.

"Is this what you're looking for?" he asked.

I grabbed my wallet and said, "Yes." I walked toward the exit.

"Don't you want to go upstairs with me?" he asked.

"No," I said firmly as I left the theater.

I left the theater, vowing that I would never return there. When I left the Cinegay, I felt relieved about my decision to do so. I had come to view the place as a mental and social "sewer." I realized that many of the patrons were not the sophisticated, articulate people I had known all my life. Initially, I regretted having frequented the place. Then, in a few months, I realized the educational factor of the theater. I realized that I probably would not have matured so fast sexually and mentally if I had not made the Cinegay a part of my life. I decided that the theater would no longer be a regular part of my life, but I felt that I could return there occasionally to watch the movies which I always enjoyed.

After a six-month absence from the theater, I returned to my former "home away from home." The patrons ranged from the desperately lonely to the seemingly well-adjusted cruiser. Still, I felt overpowered by the forced matching of couples who had sex in their seats or in the cubicles upstairs. Some patrons went home without having had sex with anyone. Those were the kinds of people I had picked up in my cruising days. I felt sorry for these new strangers. I was not about to take anyone upstairs, but I silently wished these men better luck in their subsequent visits to the Cinegay. I knew that the less obviously attractive men were often the most proficient sexually. They were just left out of the mainstream because of their looks. I hoped for their sakes that some sensitive person like me would appreciate this fact and take the lonely men into the cubicles.

About six months before I left the Cinegay, I began to frequent a gay strip bar down the street named the Bare Facts. I usually had a drink or two there, before I hit the Cinegay. I was feeling guilty about engaging in gay sex, so I drank a Scotch or two to bolster my courage for the anticipated evening of sex. At the Bare Facts, I grew to know the three male strippers on a first-name basis. I knew the two bartenders equally well.

After my visit to the Cinegay, I usually returned to the Bare Facts to get drunk and wash away my guilt about having just engaged in promiscuous, anonymous sex. I also got to watch the dancers. I became so well known at the bar that I did not have to tell the two bartenders what I wanted to drink. They automatically produced a light beer when I sat at their side of the bar. I often cruised the bar patrons, and, occasionally, I went to a nearby hotel for sex with a willing trick.

My cruising centered at the Bare Facts from the time I left the Cinegay in early October 1982, until about four weeks later, on Halloween weekend. I met a construction worker who aroused me very much with his masculine good looks. I took him home for the night. He pretended to be very tired and drunk. In frustration, I allowed him to sleep with me without sex. During the night, the man awakened and removed $30.00 of the $34.00 in my wallet. I was not aware of the theft until after he had left my apartment. I was furious and also felt somewhat foolish that I had trusted him.

Three nights later I met the same man at the Bare Facts.

"You stole my money," I protested.

"I'm real sorry," he said. "I was short of cash. I'll meet you back here tomorrow with the money I took. It's pay day tomorrow, and I promise to pay you back." I was skeptical, but I was very lonely and gullable so I accepted his story and apology.

Jerry, the man who had taken my money, introduced me to the man sitting next to him as his younger brother Billy. "I'm awfully sorry about what Jerry did to you the other night," Billy said. "I chewed his ass out real good when he got home and told me what he had done." I believed Billy's story. He continued, "Let's go to your place and have a 'three-way.' We want to make it up to you for what Jerry did."

"All right," I said, "but first let's go dancing at Nancy's."

While at Nancy's, we ran across a very drunken twenty-one-year-old named Joe. Jerry and I took pity on him and convinced Billy we would take Joe home to my place to sober him up with some of my food. The four of us arrived at my apartment, whereupon Billy retired to my bedroom to sleep. Jerry and I fed Joe some bacon and eggs. He felt somewhat better but wanted to go home. It was approximately 2:00 A.M. when Jerry and I drove Joe home in my car. I poured Joe into his apartment, saying to his brother-in-law, who opened the door, "I'm sorry, Joe is kind of drunk."

Jerry had said that he would wait for me in my car, which was parked nearby. He wanted me to leave the keys so he could play the radio. My ever sharpening street sense told me not to do so. I pocketed the keys without any comment. I returned to the car to find that Jerry had disappeared. I instantly became fearful, since I knew that we had left Billy sleeping in my apartment. I drove home to find that Billy had left, taking with him my full-length man's mink coat I had purchased in 1980, a brand new down parka, two Filipino shirts my parents had given me, and a pair of brightly colored golf pants. I felt emotionally and materially raped! "How could I have trusted those bastards?" I thought. "Fool!" It was 4:00 A.M. by then. I was exhausted and depressed. I decided to get some sleep before reporting the theft to the police.

I slept fitfully for only three hours before calling the police. The officer who took the report was polite and professional about the matter, but also extremely nervous to be in my presence. I ignored his fidgeting with his wedding ring and his numerous comments about his wife. He suggested that I call my insurance company, since the fur and the rest of the clothes were insured.

On calling the insurance company, I was referred to the claims department by my regular agent. The lady I talked with was absolutely delightful! She began our conversation in a very proper business voice, occasionally listened silently as I related how I had had only "one man" in my apartment for the evening. (I did not feel that it was necessary to advise Mrs. Shapiro that I had planned an orgy of four men that never occurred.) She carefully listed all the clothing that had been stolen.

"Mr. Simmons, I don't know you from Adam," she said, "but may I give you a Jewish grandmother's advice?" I was too tired and depressed to argue.

"Okay," I said. Mrs. Shapiro adopted a strong Yiddish accent she had not used before:

"Next time, sweetheart, go to his place!"

I roared with laughter. "Thank you," I said, "you've just

broken my depression." I was secretly pleased I had told the officer and Mrs. Shapiro the theft was gay related. It was the first time I had admitted to myself or anyone else I had done something homosexual.

The police never found Jerry or Billy. I did not anticipate that their search would be successful, since I had only the thieves' first names (which might have been aliases). I had also not secured their addresses or telephone numbers.

I notified John, one of the bartenders at the Bare Facts, about the two thefts. He told the owner, Ted. Both men agreed that, if I ever spotted Jerry or Billy at the bar, I would ask John for a Stroh's beer instead of my usual light beer. That would be John's cue to call the police. I kept the police report folded up inside my wallet for a month, in case Jerry or Billy ever returned to the Bare Facts. But they never did come back.

I was vulnerable to those two people, as I was to most people, because I met them during a devastating twelve-month period in my life in 1980. The deaths of Frank and my grandmother Simmons, which I have already mentioned, were only two of an unbelievable twenty which occurred during that year! As people dropped like flies around me, I became more reclusive at the Cinegay or in my apartment. I attended seven of the twenty funerals; I simply did not have the strength to attend the other thirteen.

In August 1980 I had purchased the fur coat which was later stolen. I also bought an expensive new car three days after I bought the coat. I did not have the money for these items, but I needed to do something dramatic to ease my troubled mind; at that point, eight people had died that year. These expensive "gifts" I gave myself kept me sane while the other twelve people died during the duration of that year.

On December 31, 1980, when Mary Kane—a fairly close friend of mine—died, I decided that I would stop counting the number of deaths among my acquaintances and start counting the number of people left alive in my circle in the greater Chicago area. I realized that day that the living people I still knew numbered nine! I felt terribly lonely, but I was determined to survive. I had my restored faith in God to give me strength, and a source of future friends through the people I still knew. I did feel he was carring me through my trauma. I was gratefull.

Shortly after New Year's Day, 1981, I called Mrs. Shaw, the mother of my sister-in-law Linda, one of my remaining friends. I told her about the terrible year I had just been through. She was shocked, but quietly and without faltering she referred me to Northminster Fellowship at the Fourth Presbyterian Church of Chicago. There I would meet new people and make some friends when I needed them most.

I latched onto "Northies" like a fish taking to water. My first visit to the group saw me extremely nervous and shy. I was scared about making a new beginning, but I was determined to leave behind forever the consuming loneliness which made my life miserable. By the time I completed my second visit to "Northies," I felt like a regular member of the group. I befriended Arlene and Brian, who became close friends outside the group. I even attended their wedding in 1983.

The group is designed for heterosexual single adults to meet and socialize. I saw no problem about joining such a group, since I still wanted to be straight. There I met and began to date Pam. She was a former City of Chicago cab driver turned auto mechanic. I was somewhat startled by her unorthodox work background, but I admired her fierce independance, which matched mine. We dated for five months, from January to June 1981.

I liked Pam until I realized that her independence was really a from of mental brutality and male emasculation. She acted "hard as nails" around men. I began to wonder what on earth I had seen in her. Pam was not very popular because of her aggressive behavior. One night she arrived at my apartment uninvited. It was about 10:00 P.M., and I had already gotten into my pajamas and bathrobe after a long, tiring day at the office. I was not in the mood for company, especially Pam's intense, combative nature. She arrived wearing my favorite perfume.

"I want to have sex with you," she said in a passionate voice.

"I don't. I'm tired," I responded honestly. But Pam would not take no for an answer. She began to untie my bathrobe and reached for the buttons on my pajama shirt. I pulled away.

"I'm really tired, and I wish you would go home," I said.

"Oh, come on, Jeremy," she persisted. She reached for my bed clothes, which I only pulled more tightly around me. Pam finally accepted the fact that I would not have sex with her. "At least you can give me a drink," she said ungraciously. I obliged her with one Scotch as we sat on the couch together in the television room.

Before I knew it, Pam and I were locked in each other's arms. She removed her blouse and bra so that I could play with her large, firm, round breasts. She became very excited. I realized, however, that I was not the least bit interested in her sexually. I stood up and announced firmly:

"I'm sorry I led you on just now. Get dressed and leave immediately!"

"You're sick, Jeremy!" Pam said as she dressed. I walked her to the front door.

"Goodbye forever, Jeremy," Pam said as she opened the door and left.

"Goodbye," I said to the now closed door.

With Pam's departure, I realized that I no longer feared sexual relations with women; I understood that I was simply not interested in them. I accepted my gay orientation which had become more and more important to me even while I was dating Pam. I decided that I would devote my full attention to leading a gay-oriented life. "To Hell with what people might think about my being gay," I thought. "Besides, all the people who might care if I'm gay are dead!"

It was June 1981 when I decided to put aside my fears of what other people might think about my sexual orientation. I decided that I must be true to my own feelings. I was extremely frightened and uncertain about my future, but I knew that I must pursue it. "I was born gay," I reasoned. "God put me into this world as a homosexual. Now I must live that kind of life." I did not feel comfortable with the idea of being gay, but at least I realized that I had no other choice.

While dating Pam, I had been frequenting the Cinegay Theater and also watching my gay home movies. My separation from Pam gave me the freedom to pursue the kind of life I was destined to lead with my gay male friends. I am not saying that I don't like women; I only want them as nonsexual friends. All of the women in my life today know that I am gay. We are extremely close, regardless of my sexual orientation.

Later in 1981, I realized how much I hated working at Simmons and Quigley. I felt the oppressive atmosphere of the office to be stifling to my burgeoning mental independence and related gay-oriented feelings. I loved my father, and I still do. I simply did not want to work with him any longer. We had built up a marvelous bond of mutual trust and respect. My major regrets about working with him were the facts that I did not appreciate his reading and editing every letter I wrote, and the very demanding people with whom I had to work every day at the condominiums and cooperatives I managed. I felt tortured by the numerous personalities I had to please. It seemed that the harder I tried to please the customers the more demanding they became. They were apartment owners, so I figured that I could not protest too loudly without risking losing the accounts and my job. Furthermore, I resented earning only $12,000 per year after ten years on the job. I did not fully appreciate how much more valuable my services were, but I was certain that they were worth more than that. I shopped around for a new job until I landed one with Bruce at Keynote Realty. My starting pay was $20,000 per year. My new boss was the first person not to ask, "Why did you want to leave a family-owned company?" I was far too bashful to cite the above reasons for my decision. I simply made appointments with as many potential employers as possible, until I met Bruce.

My new friend met me and hired me on the spot. "Freedom at last to live my own life!" I thought. I could live my life as a homosexual without any fear of my parents' interference in my life, I reasoned. Then my father dropped his bombshell. He was selling Simmons and Quigley to Harold Quiqley and joining me at Keynote Realty! I was stunned.

I enjoyed my new job at first, depite Dad's presense, but my pleasure quickly turned to despair and frustration when I realized that only a few people at the office really cared about the quality of our work. Bruce gave his employees little support in fighting the uncaring company officers who occupied more senior positions than we did. They allowed the computer department to be staffed by incompetent people who did not know how to program the hardware properly.

As a result of poorly programmed computers, monthly financial reports were mailed to owners which reflected inaccurate dollar amounts of income and expenses for the various buildings we managed. The accounts receivable department, which processed the incoming rent and assessment checks, improperly credited the tenants' accounts. Other clerical errors by employees who did not care about their jobs went unchecked in most cases. It was the daily battle with the bureaucracy of the company that forced me to resign in complete frustration only nine months after I joined Keynote. I now also wanted to separate from my father.

The company was headed toward bankruptcy, which was a further incentive for me to "bail out" before the corporate ship sank totally. In June 1982, I found a new corporate home with Briarcliff Realty. I worked there for thirteen months, enjoying myself very much. I did have to get used to working in a very small office; there were only five of us. The mood was laid-back. Jane and Tom Higgins owned and operated the office. They were fun, relaxed people who did not believe in dressing in coats and ties for work. This job, therefore, was the first I had had where I was encouraged to dress casually for work. I slowly bought the necessary blue jeans, casual slacks and sports shirts I needed to fit in with the dress style of the office.

Tom and Jane's relaxed attitude about taking it easy during the day to pace oneself was a revelation to me. I had previously been a "workaholic" who rushed to complete every task. It was a somewhat uneasy transition for me as I learned to slow down and begin to enjoy myself at work, but I eventually adapted to my new surroundings. I worked with my friends for thirteen months, leaving only because I felt that I was not earning enough money to survive financially. We parted the best of friends.

While at Briarcliff, I also worked with a very nice man named Fred. He and my other fellow workers were all in their late twenties, while I was the "grandfather" of the place at thirty-three. Fred used to get mildly irritated when I raced around the office emptying wastepaper baskets and generally tidying up the place. We had no maid service, and I have always hated dirt and clutter.

"You must be gay," Fred joked to me one day. "You keep this place so neat and clean." At the time I did not take his remark as a joke.

Off the top of my head, I shot back through clenched teeth, "I am!"

Fred gasped, embarrassed, "God, I'm sorry. I didn't mean anything by my comment." I could tell that he meant what he was saying. The entire exchange took place in front of Jane and Tom.

Jane responded happily, "I had a gay male roommate at Northwestern for four years." I was startled but pleased.

Although Tom did not speak nor looked surprised, he was supportive. He tried to ignore my outburst as unimportant in our working relationship. "Jeremy," he said, "please help me with this project I'm working on." I was deeply grateful that Tom did not even bat an eyelash at my comment, and even more grateful that he showed his continuing support of me by asking me to work on a building financial report he was having trouble figuring out.

Outside the office, Fred, his wife Sarah, Tom and Jane routinely socialized with me. Soon after I let it be known that I was gay, Tom and Jane invited me to one of their parties. "Bring a friend," Jane said warmly. She knew that I would bring a male companion. Al, my lover at the time, joined me for an after-dinner party at Sarah and Fred's home. There were about twenty people at the party. Most of the people present knew that Al and I were gay; absolutely nobody seemed to care. We were accepted as equals, which pleased me tremendously.

At work or socializing with Sarah, Fred, Tom and Jane, I quickly learned I wasn't encouraged to discuss my private life. They simply didn't want to know. Intellectually I could accept their wishes. Emotionally, however, I felt like an excited child wanting to share my new adventures. I allowed my more mature sense of reason to control my silence. I considered my friends mature beyond their years. I was disapointed to realize they still weren't interested in learning about my life experiences.

All my life I have felt comfortable in the presence of older or mature people. I readily gravitated to older men for sex. The ideal candidate was twenty to twenty-five years my senior. I discovered that my natural preference for such men made me an inter-generational homosexual. Such relationships were not like father and son, but like older brother/younger brother. Many younger men in the gay community are leery of such relationships. Some younger gay men fear the effects of the aging process. I delight in it. Older men are often perceived as impotent, but I have discovered only one such older man who was not good in bed. Many younger gays describe older ones as "unattractive." I have met many older men in their fifties and sixties, however, who routinely take care of their bodies. They arouse me greatly.

While I frequented the Cinegay, I had sex with perhaps five hundred or six hundred men over a two-year period. Approximately half of them were over fifty. I preferred their personalities and sexual abilities to those of men aged twenty-one to forty-nine. The younger group was, as a rule, less secure in its sexual orientation than the older group. There were exceptions to people's maturity and desirability in all age groups, but—by and large—I would have to say that gays who adamantly refuse to associate sexually or socially with older men are short-changing themselves from a potentially rewarding experience.

There is already too much ageism in the world at large. The

gay community does not need to emulate this unfortunate facet of culture in general. I have noted that I *lust* after handsome young men, i.e. the dancers and bartenders I meet at the Bare Facts. Some of these men are even good friends. However, the warm, caring and lasting relationships I tend to make are with less physically attractive, but equally delightful, older men in their forties and up.

The "middle-aged group" of men, from thirty to fifty, are likely to be in various stages of their mental development in accepting themselves as homosexuals. They may or may not feel totally comfortable about engaging in homosexual intercourse. Frankly, the most sexually proficient men I have met are usually over fifty. Again, there are always exceptions to this rule.

CHAPTER 5
The Butterfly Emerges

By 1982, I was devoting most of my social life to gay-oriented events. I still did not have many friends except for the nine "stalwarts" from 1980. I had been receiving gay movies and magazines at home through the mail. I realized that I had spent about $3,000 on such material, to date, and decided that I did not need to keep spending my money at such a terrible rate. I stopped ordering new material; the immediate result of that action was the removal of my name from the lists of the half dozen or so companies which sent me fliers. I then discarded the movie projector I had purchased for the films. I did not want to be tempted to buy any more movies, since they began to bore me after only a couple of viewings.

Besides, I figured that I was seeing all the action I wanted and needed at the Cinegay and at the Bare Facts. I noticed that I was now drinking heavily. That concerned me, since I did not want to be an alcoholic like my parents. I decided to label myself an alcoholic now, although I refused to attend any AA meetings. I discovered that I liked to drink which I did in fits and starts. I felt guilty about being gay, which depressed me, and about engaging in gay sex, which depressed me even more. I drank to "feel better" and to be less inhibited publicly. I also thought my drinking would magically remove my negative feeling. It never did. In fact, I felt worse. I guess I just have to excert more control over my life.

One night in 1982, I was drinking heavily at the Bare Facts. The beer I had consumed did not dull my mind as it usually did. I found myself immersed in mental anguish about being gay. I thought, "Why me, Lord? Why did You make me gay? My life could have been so much easier if You'd made me straight." To my depression was added anger.

Years later, in 1984, I would realize that when my Maker

made me a homosexual, He also gave me the strength to be socially different. God also showed me, through the examples of other gay men and women, how wonderful and fulfilling a life gays of both sexes can live. I am now glad that God made me the person I am. My adjustment to being gay has not been easy, but I truly believe that the Lord gave me a special gift when He made me gay.

To this point I had kept my sexual orientation secret from most people I knew. Only three very close business associates—two at Simmons and Quigley, one at Keynote Realty—knew that I was gay. So far I had not had the dramatic encounter at Briarcliff with Jane, Tom and Fred to which I referred in the last chapter. The reaction of my three former business associates was completely calm and supportive. I still felt very guilty and nervous about having told them that I was gay, but I was pleased by their reaction to the news.

My closest friend outside the Cinegay who knew that I was gay was a dancer named Jim. He worked at the Bare Facts. I suspect that he could see how troubled I was about being gay. He once told me, "Jeremy, it'll take you another year to settle into the idea that you're gay." I was shocked and angered. I thought, "I've already taken twenty years to accept the fact that I'm gay. I can't wait another year!" But Jim's observation turned out to be accurate.

Jim is a very unusual man. He is twenty-nine years old at present. In 1983 he retired as a dancer and became one of the two evening bartenders. I frequent the Bare Facts weekly to visit with Jim, who is an extraordinarily good-looking blond with an athletic build from regular workouts with weights. I initially lusted after his body. Now, I admire his physique, but consider him to be a very good friend rather than a potential lover. We have socialized together at my apartment on several occasions. The first time he visited me, he said, "Jeremy, I don't usually see Bare Facts customers outside the bar. You're different. I like you, and I know I can trust you to be my friend." I was quite flattered by his comment. He was right: I would never take advantage of our friendship.

Jim is an unusually articulate man. He is tending bar at night, but during the day he is attending college, where he majors in physical education. He intends to become a corporate adviser to major firms that want to start company athletic groups. Such groups are now becoming big business. Jim will establish new groups for companies and help the executives find qualified employees to run the programs he starts.

Jim gave up dancing because he felt like a mindless piece of "prime beef" while on stage. He hated to be exploited by ogling male customers who generally did not get to know him offstage. In contrast, I have made it a point to become acquainted with each of the employees at the Bare Facts on a personal basis. We are not close, but at least the men know that I am not there just to watch them dance.

Since going to college Jim has learned German. I understand a few words of the language and can make an occasional response to his comments when I understand them. We enjoy thanking each other and saying "You're welcome" in German. Some of the other patrons at the bar seem impressed by the fact that we can converse even sparingly in a language other than English.

Sometimes I cannot think of an appropriate response when Jim says something to me in German. I immediately lapse into French on such occasions, since I speak that language fluently. Jim does not speak French, but I have taught him a few key phrases, including "You're welcome" and "Do you want to go to bed with me tonight?" Jim knows that that last question is not serious, but he always answers me with a firm "Nein!"

The two years I have spent at the Bare Facts so far have been instrumental in the psychological changes I have undergone. Seeing the guys' exposed bodies, I have lost all residual fears I had about my own body. I no longer feel that the human body is "dirty" or "sinful" when exposed. Since I began to frequent the Bare Facts, I have allowed Jim and one other dancer, Peter, to wrap their arms or legs around my head and face when I deliberately sit on a barstool next to the runway the dancers use. Both men have

111

told me that I and a select few other regular patrons are "trustworthy" enough for them to make such provocative gestures. I certainly enjoyed the feel of my friends' bodies wrapped around me. I also appreciated their confidence in me, which I would never abuse.

When Jim was dancing he would strip. He covered his genitals with a straw cowboy hat. He did a "bump and grind" to the blaring music while allowing me to hold his hat in place with my hand. Only once did I accidentally let the hat slip. Jim realized that the slip was unintentional and let me continue to hold his hat when he did his routine.

During the two years that I have been writing this book (1982-84), I have given Jim two different copies of the manuscript. He knows everything there is to know about me, and has reciprocated by telling me much about himself. We are close as two people could be. My only concern is that our friendship has centered back at the Bare Facts. I hope that, when Jim reads this version of my book, he will appreciate the sincerity I feel about our friendship. If there are any barriers to socialization between us outside the Bare Facts, I hope that he will tell me. I would like us to see each other regularly at his apartment and at mine, so that we can build upon the affection I believe to be mutual.

In October 1981 I began to believe that I must come out to my friends. I was drinking heavily during the entire time (about a year) I was mulling over the question of how to perform that task. I was terrified by the prospect of what my remaining friends would think and say about me. Despite the fact that I was frequenting the Cinegay Theater and the Bare Facts, I still felt as if I were the only homosexual in the world. I had no idea that dozens of counselling services and gay social organizations already existed. They were there waiting to help me and other unresolved gays.

In October 1982 I "exploded" from the closet! I no longer cared what the world thought; I wanted everyone to know that I was gay. I was still feeling scared, but I felt that I could no longer live my life in secrecy and shame. I wrote my pen pal, Marie, a heterosexual woman I had befriended in 1970. She was the former girlfriend of my good friend Ed at Bellwood Academy. Marie and I have corresponded monthly for the last ten years.

Ed and Marie met while he was a student at Yale and she was a student at Mt. Holyoke College nearby. Marie is from Boston. She lives there now with her husband and year-old daughter. Ed has since moved to the Los Angeles area where he remains a bachelor.

Marie's reaction to the news that I was gay was nothing short of spectacular. We philosophized about my alternate lifestyle. "Many gays and straights have the same problems in life," Marie once wrote to me. "Everyone should be more tolerant of each other." Over the years, Marie and I have exchanged some extremely confidential messages. Those confidences remain intact for both of us and will do so until we die.

Ken, another heterosexual friend from Boston, heard the news that I was gay when he visited me in Chicago in October 1982. He smiled broadly and shook my hand. "My sister's gay," he responded. I was staggered by that news. I had thought I was the only upper middle class gay person in the world. "Human sexual orientation has no barriers in race, color, creed or family background," Ken said. I was very pleased. Ken's family lives in Lewisberg Square, a place considered by many Bostonians to be the most exclusive part of Beacon Hill. I have since met Ken's sister Trudy. She is a delightful person two years younger than I. Trudy and her lover, Lois, share a house in the suburbs of Boston. Ken and Trudy's parents have accepted their daughter's lifestyle and her lover. Lois routinely joins Trudy for visits in Boston.

As I received positive feedback from my straight friends who lived outside Chicago, I grew stronger and happier about the fact that I was gay. I grew to the point that I did not want to remain silent about my sexual orientation. I felt great to be alive! I next told some of my heterosexual friends from Chicago that I was gay. Most of them accepted the information without qualms. Three people did make excuses of "being too busy" or not calling back when I phoned them. I no longer see those people, but I am not resentful of their fears. I feel that their lack of acceptance of me as a person is their problem rather than mine. I hope that in time they will come to understand that people can lead different lifestyles which do not necessarily threaten or make less valuable either person's existence in the world.

Probably the most valuable heterosexual friend I have retained is my minister, Father Boyle. I came out to him during a luncheon to which he invited me near our church. "I'm gay, Father," I said nervously when he asked me what I was doing socially in my life. He and Mrs. Boyle were two of the remaining nine friends I had after the many deaths in 1980. They knew of my extreme loneliness and were concerned about my efforts to rebuild my social life. "I'm centering my life in mostly gay social settings."

"Thank you for sharing that news with me, Jeremy," Father Boyle said. "Are you aware that before Mrs. Boyle and I moved to Chicago I ministered to the gay community in Berkeley, California?"

"No," I said, delighted. I later discovered that Father Boyle is a member of the Board of Directors of a local gay academic group here in Chicago. He continues to minister, as a heterosexual, to his gay brothers and sisters in Chicago.

"We are all God's children," Father Boyle went on to say. "He loves all of us." I was overwhelmed with relief that I had such a sensitive, understanding friend in my minister.

The first Tuesday in December 1982, I attended my first Mattachine Midwest meeting. This group is the oldest gay men's discussion group in Chicago. It was founded in 1964. I read about it in an advertisement in *Gay Life*, which invited all interested gay men to join the discussion group every Tuesday night. I nervously went to the meeting site at the designated time.

I was afraid that the place might cater to more "streetwise" gay men, like the ones I knew well at the Cinegay and the Bare Facts. I did not know if more sophisticated people existed, but I felt that there was no harm in my finding out. I sat in silent terror, feeling wretched because I was gay, as I listened to the more experienced members of the group participate in the evening's discussion.

Almost immediately, however, I realized that I was in the company of some wonderful people. These were not at all like the hustlers and low grade people I knew at the Bare Facts or the Cinegay. Tears filled my eyes as I thought, "I've come home to the gay community and to myself!" I remained silent as I listened to the balance of the evening's discussion. For the first time in my life, I realized that it was good to be gay. Homosexuality was no longer something "dirty" or "sick." Very quickly I became proud of the fact that I am gay.

I got to the point that I could not wait for the next week's discussion group meeting. The topics of conversation changed weekly. Five different members of the group would host the meetings on a rotating basis. In time I was invited to become one of the discussion "facilitators." I felt deeply honored as I accepted the invitation. It is our responsibility to think up topics of discussion for the weekly meetings and to encourage other members to submit topics for discussion. My leadership qualities and related ease about chairing groups of approximately twenty people grew very strong. I felt comfortable in my role as one of the leaders of our group.

Later in December I was scheduled to visit my parents at their winter home in Florida. I did so, but decided in advance that they too must know that I am gay. We had alluded to the possibility during our Thanksgiving dinner together in Lake Forest before my parents flew south for the winter.

I was too nervous to pick up the phone to confirm the information that I was gay. Instead I wrote my parents a letter, feeling that I would think more slowly and less emotionally when writing things down, which is characteristic of me.

"Dear Mom and Dad,

I've been wanting to tell you this news for a long time. I'm a homosexual. Please don't hate me. God knows, I've done enough of that for all of us during the last twenty years.

I love you both very much, and I'm looking forward to

seeing you next week in Key West.

Love,

Jeremy"

My hands shook as I mailed the letter. The phone rang two days later in my apartment. It was my parents.

"You got the letter," I told my father.

"What letter?" he asked.

"Oh, no!" I said. "You should be getting a letter from me in the mail soon. In it I told you that I'm gay." There was a long pause.

My father finally said, softly, "You're what?"

"I'm gay, Dad. I wanted you and Mom to know before I got to Key West later this week." My mother had been listening to the entire conversation.

"We love you, Jeremy," she said.

"Yes, son, we do love you," my father echoed.

I arrived in Key West during the day on Christmas Eve, 1982. My parents picked me up at the airport. My father hugged me, something he had last done when I had announced my attempted suicide at college at the age of eighteen. Mom hugged and kissed me warmly. They looked troubled.

"Wolfgang (the family's German shepherd) had to be put to sleep yesterday. Your Aunt Midge (Mom's sister) died two days ago," my father commented tersely.

"Gosh, I'm sorry," I said, thinking to myself, "And my letter arrived only the day before Aunt Midge died. I said aloud, "What a week you two have had!"

My brother Allan and his girlfriend Alice were in town for the holidays. Mom and Dad had told them about my letter. Dad had even invited Allan to read it. I did not mind that he had done so, since I intended to come out to them during my stay in Key West. Allan was visibly upset about my news.

"Well! You've certainly ruined Alice's and *my* vacation!" he said. "Bullshit!" I shot back. "You know as well as I do that Aunt Midge's death and Wolfgang's termination would have had the same effect on them." Allan lowered his head.

"You're right," he said. "Well, at least your lifestyle certainly isn't mine!" I greeted my brother's ire in silence.

Allan and I went on to discuss my homosexuality in private.

"Dad's awfully upset, Jeremy," Allan said. "You might want to ease his mind by telling him that your sexuality isn't a central issue in your life."

"But it is," I interrupted.

"Tell him anyway," Allan pressed. I felt confused. Allan added, "Dad's worried about what his friends might think if they know you're gay."

"That's crazy," I said. "Dad didn't make me gay. I was born this way."

"Still, he's worried," Allan said. "Tell him." That night, in an effort to assuage my father's obvious concern about me, I lied to him and said that my sexual orientation was not the driving force in my life.

"Good!" Dad said with a sigh of relief. "You could be badly hurt by your lifestyle." We engaged in a very intense and personal discussion, parts of which my mother also heard. The three of us stayed home instead of going to midnight Christmas Eve services at church.

My father concluded the conversation by saying quite dramatically, "I've failed you as a father!"

"No, you didn't," I said earnestly. "You and Mom had absolutely nothing to do with my being gay. It just happened. Now I'm beginning to feel good about it."

The next day Mom took me aside in the living room.

"Thank you for writing the letter," she said. "Dad and I love you very much. We're concerned about your being happy. If you're happy, then that's what counts. Please know that I love you very much."

"Thank you, Mom," I said. "I *am* happy."

"Good," she said. "By the way, I suspected you were gay for the last ten years."

"Now you know," I said.

"Right," Mom smiled. We hugged and kissed each other.

It has taken my parents a year and a half to accept me as their gay son. That they do so now is evidenced by their asking me to invite my friends to join us for meals together in Lake Forest. My father does not like to discuss the topic of homosexuality, but he graciously accepts the presence of my friends when they join me for our visits.

As a result of my mother's unfaltering support of me since I came out to her, she and I have at last become good friends. She accepts me as an adult, and no longer as her "baby" (a term that always distanced me from her emotionally in my adult years). My feelings that she had never wanted me to be born are gone, and I know that she loves me very much. I now love her equally in return. We are developing a closeness that, I suspect, will never wane again. As I was growing up, I did not realize how genuine a friend my mother was; I permitted myself to discover that fact only when I became a gay adult.

Mark and Linda learned that I was gay when their daughter was born in early December 1982. I was feeling jealous of their marriage and family which seemed more socially acceptable than my own lifestyle. I came out to Mark at his home the day my niece, their second child, was born.

"You know," he said, "Linda is deeply involved with Dignity International (a gay Catholic organization). She hosted a symposium on lesbian rights when she was eight months pregnant with your nephew." (My nephew was their firstborn child.)

"No, I didn't know," I answered. "That's great!"

Linda has, indeed, been my strongest supporter, especially in comparison with her husband, my brother. Although Mark seemed to accept my news at the time I came out to him, his enthusiasm has ebbed and flowed during the last eighteen months. He supports my right to live my life as I must, but I get the distinct impression that he wishes I were straight. However, Mark and Linda invite me and my friends to their house about half the time that we visit each other. I would prefer that they allowed me to bring a friend all the time, but they do not agree with that point of view. I once commented, "If I were dating a woman, I bet you'd let her join me every time I visited you." Mark agreed with my point. Linda was more reserved, saying, "I might not want her in my home if I did not like her." Mark, Linda and I have reached an agreement to the effect that I may bring a male friend when visiting them at times when no other guests are present. My niece and nephew always socialize with me whether I visit their home alone or with a friend. I hope that the children will grow up to realize that people need not be segregated because of their sexual orientation. My parents similarly entertain me with my friends when no other guests are present.

After I came out to myself and to my friends and family, I began to learn the greater implications of being gay. I discovered there are social and health concerns that all responsible people share—namely the control of venereal disease and the treatment of one social group by another. I quickly discovered the epidemic of A.I.D.S., gonorrhea, hepatitis, herpes, and syphilis. I quickly went to the local gay owned and operated clinic in Chicago which tests gay men and women for such diseases. I realized that in the two years I had been sexually active, I had never considered the possibility of my contracting such illnesses. I had been reading reports in *Gay Life* that approximately 80% of all A.I.D.S. patients die from the disease. I did not know if I was even infected.

Happily, all of my tests proved negative. I felt God had performed a miracle in keeping me healthy. During my battery of tests, I requested that the doctor test my blood for antibodies to hepatitis B. The disease is not fatal, but it can make the patient very sick. I discovered I had no antibodies to hepititis, so I immediately signed up to receive the three prescribed vaccinations that usually produce an immunity to the disease. Now, I regularly visit the clinic for my semiannual STD test (sexually transmitted disease test).

Sadly, not every gay man and woman gets tested. Some people are afraid of the possible results. Others think they will not get sick. I cannot emphasize strongly enough the need for EVERY sexually active gay man or woman to be tested regularly. The cost of such tests is not great when compared to the possible hospital expenses if one becomes ill. Also, the local clinic in Chicago (and I imagine in other major cities across America) will take into account the personal finances of any person who cannot afford to pay the regular cost of such examinations.

There is indescribable mental relief knowing you are healthy. Also, your sex partners can rest assured that the chances of their getting infected by you are greatly reduced when you have sex together. Sex is an integral part of a human being's life. It should be enjoyed to the fullest. My friends and I enjoy our sexual times together, but we do not hesitate to inquire discreetly of each other if we have any known diseases that might be contagious. I realize some people are reluctant to bring up such a delicate question before having sex, but I figure we gays can be mature about the subject and accept our partner's concern in order to assure our mutual good health and enjoyment of sex. When we do have sex we use condoms or engage in "safe sex" practices.

One potential sex partner of mine was honest enough to confide that he has a chronic version of hepatitis B. This unusual form of the disease never ceases to be contagious to people without antibodies. We avoided having sex together until I knew that I had sufficient antibodies to ward off his infection. The doctor assures me there is little or no danger of my ever contracting the disease from my friend. I still see my friend from time to time, although we no longer engage in sex together, for reasons totally unrelated to his infection.

Other aspects of the gay community I discovered related to the treatment of gays and non-gays towards one another. I learned that many gays segregate themselves from their heterosexual counterparts. Some homosexuals have experienced harassment and general nonacceptance by the more homophobic members of the straight community. Similarly, some heterosexuals have encountered heterophobic gays who occasionally discriminate against them at work. One such example includes a straight friend of mine who could not get a musical book published because her gay acquaintance somehow blocked its publication.

Vindictiveness by either the gay or straight community is cruel and unnecessary. Neither camp benefits from such experiences. Only lingering resentment and fears of both communities result, keeping the members apart socially and mentally. Sadly, there are discriminatory people in both the gay and straight cultures. Some gays hate straights because of their sexual orientation, and for no other reason. Other gays hate members of their same community because of their race or social background. Such similarities extend into the heterosexual community. The sooner ALL people realize we are fellow human beings, the sooner we can begin to break down the mental and social barriers that continue to separate us.

CHAPTER 6
Freedom

The first fact I discovered about being gay is that one never stops "coming out" until the day one dies. Every day I feel more relaxed and normal about the fact that I am gay. My sexual orientation is as integral a part of me as my respiratory system. In December 1982 I was flushed with excitement and happiness that I had accepted myself as a homosexual. I wanted the world to know that I was gay. I also wanted to settle down with one gay lover for the rest of my life. I thought that that was the only way to live.

In the Mattachine discussion group there was an older man named Al. I was much impressed by his articulate nature and wit. Although he had a rather caustic and opinionated side to his nature, I did not care. He was not like Pam, whom I had met at "Northies." While letting loose with opinions which were controversial, he could be quite gentle.

In March 1983 I was undergoing some personal financial difficulty. I needed a roommate to share my expenses. I considered Al a natural choice for a roommate and invited him to move in immediately. He warned me that he, too, was undergoing some financial problems, but I did not care. I thought that whatever help he could give me financially would be better than nothing. It turned out that he was in even more serious financial trouble than I was; this troubled me, but I was not ready to ask him to move out. I had permanent company which prevented me from feeling lonely. In a very few weeks I discovered that I was supporting both of us on my reduced income. I was working at Briarcliff Realty, and the commissions I was earning were barely getting us by.

Within forty-eight hours of the time Al moved in with me, he fell madly in love with me. I was mesmerized by his beguiling ways and believed that I shared his love. We catapulted into an intense emotional and physical relationship. The seriousness of the relationship did not blind me to the fact that Al was a heavy drinker, a discovery which bothered me since I was drinking almost as much as he was. About eight weeks after moving in with me, Al proposed marriage to me. I was swept off my feet. "Yes!" I blurted out impulsively. To myself I thought, "At last I will have the wedding and permanent partner I could never have had with Jean." I was ecstatic. I realize today I didn't love Al. I simply loved being in a relationship. If you will, I was "in love with love".

I contacted Father Boyle at my church to ask if he would assist at the wedding. Al and I wanted to get married at the local gay Community Church in Chicago. The rector of the church was scheduled to preside at the ceremony, necessitating Father Boyle's participation as an assistant rather than the major officiator.

Father Boyle told me some very disturbing information. He said that the Episcopal Diocese of Chicago did not sanction gay marriages since such unions are forbidden by canon law. Gay marriages may not be held in any Chicago Episcopal church, and no Episcopal priest may participate in such ceremonies. Episcopalians who did marry other people of the same sex would not be recognized or sanctioned by the church in such relationships. I was furious. The happiest day of my life could not be recognized by my church!

Happily, Father Boyle saw a loophole in church law. He told me that, if Al and I were willing to change the name of the ceremony from *wedding* to anything else, he could participate as he very much wished to do. Al and I discussed the matter and came up with the appellation "A Ceremony of Friendship and Devotion," enabling Father Boyle to participate in the service.

I approached my sister-in-law, Linda, to participate in the service. She was more reserved than Father Boyle had been. She told me that she would have to think about her decision. She was accustomed to the idea that weddings were an exclusively heterosexual event. I was hurt and surprised that Linda's otherwise liberal views on homosexuality did not apply to this glorious event in my life, but I waited patiently for her to make up her mind.

Initially, Linda and Mark decided not to attend the ceremony at all while it was called a wedding. The change in the name of the service allowed them to change their minds; Linda decided that she would not participate in the event except as a member of the congregation. I was disappointed but consoled myself with the thought that at least some of my family would be there.

Knowing that my parents would not understand what I was doing, I did not inform them of my wedding plans. I was also aware that they did not like Al. I was very sad that I could not include my entire family in an event that all heterosexual families routinely share. The difference between gay and straight living was brought home to me with a vengeance.

I did not invite Allan and Alice to the wedding, since I knew that they would not understand any more than Mom and Dad would. That had been made clear by Allan's reaction to my announcement at the time we met in Key West. Again, I was sorry that my entire family could not share my joy as I married the man I pretended I loved.

I became "social secretary" for the wedding. I ignored the fact that I would have to pay for the cost of the ceremony, the reception, our honeymoon in San Francisco and our wedding rings. While my excitement about the upcoming ceremony grew, Al remained silent. I put together a list of guests numbering one hundred fifty people, of which Al invited only half a dozen. I began to have second thoughts when I realized the ceremony would cost $3,000. "Is Al worth all this?" I asked myself. For the first time I sat down alone quietly and began to think in rational terms.

I realized that Al was broke. I had already loaned him a great deal of money so that he could pay his debts. The loan eventually became a gift, since there was no way he could ever repay me. I also realized that I was "buying" my happiness and avoiding my former loneliness by continuing to subsidize him. I began to think that he was not worth all that expense. I refused to consider that I actually didn't love him. That thought was too scary to contemplate.

I was also aware that Mark, Linda and my parents could not tolerate Al; they found him loud and boorish, and I was beginning to share their opinion. My father also pegged Al as a "gold digger" who was interested in my money rather than in me. To this day I do not believe that Al consciously sought my money; he merely relied upon me to "take care" of him, as a child would. I grew resentful, since, at the time, Al was fifty-nine while I was thirty-four and expected to take care of myself while he took care of himself.

My underlying concerns about Al and our future together interfered with the pleasure I had formerly taken in sleeping with him. We reached the point of demanding sex from each other where we had formerly engaged in the act without any prompting. The frequency of our times together also diminished from three to four times per week at the beginning to once a week during the last month we remained together. I realized I didn't enjoy having sex with my lover.

I became very much afraid of being an alcoholic, as I realized how much Al and I were drinking together. I also did not want to live with an alcoholic. Still I was afraid to ask Al to leave; drunk or not, he was company for me. Also, he had helped me to eliminate permanently my lingering fears about "sleeping with men as if to make them women" (which had been preached from Leviticus when I was young).

At one point in Al's life he had been a Presbyterian Navy chaplain. I was quite comfortable about living with a former disciple of God, although he had renounced his religion and God years ago. I discussed my concerns about the passage from Leviticus with him, telling him that I felt guilty about sleeping with men.

"Did you ever do so with the idea that they were women?" he asked.

"No!" I bellowed.

"Then you have nothing to worry about," Al said. "You never violated the tenets of the passage." I was overjoyed! I felt no more guilt feelings about being gay and engaging in gay sex.

As a teenager and a man in his early twenties, Al was a fanatical athlete. He played football and lifted weights. But the years had not been kind to his physique; in time many of his developed muscles turned soft and flabby. Since he wanted to tone up his body once again, he invited me to join him at one of the local gay bathhouses which housed Universal weight equipment. I tended to take Mark Twain's attitude about athletics. Twain once wrote: "Every time I get the urge to exercise, I go lie down until it passes." But Al would hear nothing of my sentiments or those of Mark Twain either, and so, reluctantly, I joined Al in the weight room at the bathhouse.

In a very short time I noticed that I was losing twenty pounds that I had not been able to shed earlier. I was delighted. Also, I noticed that my dyslexia did not interfere with my workouts as it had with other sports. I enjoyed the time I spent at the bathhouse with Al, although I grumbled about his over-enthusiastic urging that I work harder. The results of my increased efforts paid off. Young, handsome men were openly cruising me as I worked out in my tight-fitting silk shorts. More importantly, I felt sexy in my own right for the first time in my life. I give Al total credit for showing me the way to a good-looking body and a strong self-image.

With the wedding ceremony approaching, I wanted to include as guests all my heterosexual friends from grade school and high school. I impulsively called Marty in Boston, Paul in Santa Fe, Ed in Los Angeles, Roy in North Carolina and Chris near Chicago. I told all of them, "Are you sitting down? I'm gay, and I'm marrying a man I love very much. His name is Al. I hope you'll be able to attend the wedding." All my friends accepted the invitations!

Only after I had made the last phone call did I realize the great risk I had just taken in coming out to my friends. Any or all of them might have ceased to associate with me. I am deeply grateful that the relationships we had developed over the years precluded such a possibility and that I may rely upon my friends. Only Roy seemed to be shocked by my announcement, but he too told me that our friendship during the twenty years since high school would remain as it was. I keep in touch with him and with the others who will always be very special people in my life.

Al was also pleased by my friends' support. However, I was growing increasingly concerned about our relationship. I confronted Al with my feelings about his drinking and about our financial situation. He seemed concerned about both problems.

"I love you very much, Jeremy," he said. But I knew then that I did not love him as much as he loved me.

"Let's not get married," I suggested. Al looked hurt.

"How about if we had a smaller ceremony?" he suggested. I realized that the impending ceremony was placing a strain on our relationship that I did not want. We had only known each other for four months; perhaps we were rushing into something that might be disastrous for both of us.

I did not want to hurt Al's feelings, however, so I went ahead and ordered the invitations at the printer. That night, Al and I got very drunk and got into an argument. The subject of the argument was the financial problem we were having considering our disparity. I told Al, "You're drunk, and so am I. I'm going to bed. Maybe we'll feel different in the morning." I retired, but Al—who was a night owl—remained awake in his own bedroom with the light on. About 2:00 A.M., while going to the bathroom, I noticed that he had still not gone to bed. I looked into his room on the way to the bathroom. He was drinking Scotch right out of the bottle! I was horrified and very angry. I grabbed the bottle from his hand and poured the balance of the contents down the drain. Thoughts of my parents' alcoholism raced through my mind. "You're moving out of here in the morning," I told Al angrily. He looked dazed. He understood what I had said, but I don't think he believed me.

We went to sleep immediately after the incident. The next morning saw no change in my feelings; I was still determined to see that Al moved out. I no longer feared the possibility of being lonely again; eliminating Al from my life was the important thing.

At work, Jane and Tom were completely in favor of my decision to evict Al. "Take off as much time as you need today, Jeremy," Tom told me. I spent half the day packing Al's bags for him at home. "I don't have any place to go," Al said piteously. I made a reservation for him at the Abbott Hotel, a gay hotel in Chicago. "I don't have the room rent," Al said. I gave him a twenty-dollar bill which covered one night at the hotel.

After I finished packing Al's bags, I placed them in my car and drove him to the Abbott. The room I had reserved for him was waiting. I remained cold and calm throughout the ordeal of moving him out of my apartment, but when I got home from the drive I broke down completely and cried for hours. After I recovered, I was scared about my future but relieved that Al was no longer a part of my life.

Al and I still see each other at Mattachine meetings. We even hug and kiss each other now when we meet. He has become a friend again, but—given the difference in our personal makeups—I will never be as close to him as I was before.

After continued problems with drinking, I stopped entirely in January 1984. I am monitoring my desire to smoke, which decreases daily.

As I write this book, it is now July 1984. I have been sober since January of this year and feel basically secure in my life without alcohol. Although I was unemployed for several weeks during June and July 1984 (having lost my position at Skokie Realty, where I worked after leaving Briarcliff Realty at the end of August 1983), I had no desire to "drown my sorrows." I feel proud of the fact. I found a new position in real estate without breaking my code of sobriety.

For a month after Al and I broke up, I could not even look at, much less touch, another man. I needed time to get over my whirlwind romance. Eventually, I met Larry at a Mattachine meeting. He was a soft-spoken man aged forty-three. I was impressed that he was very sensitive and caring. We tried to be lovers for about six months in late 1983 and early 1984, but eventually decided that our nonsexual friendship was far more rewarding than any sexual relationship we might have. To this day we are extremely close. In some ways, Larry has replaced my college friend Frank as my closest friend. We have exchanged very sensitive personal secrets with each other. We can and do talk about everything and anything in complete confidence.

For a while I felt a sense of unreciprocated love for Larry, but he convinced me that I was better off falling in love with someone else. However, I doubt that I will ever love someone as much as I have loved him. Larry helped me to draw closer to my parents, who had become more detached from me since I came out to them in December 1982. Larry told me, after meeting my parents, "They're delightful! Just don't press the issue about your being gay. They already love you because you are their son. Let that be enough. You don't have to be their *gay* son." I was impressed by Larry's unassailable logic in making that point.

Since Larry and I ceased to be lovers I have come to realize that living the "single life" without a permanent lover is not a terrible alternative after all. I no longer feel desperate to pick up the first available man I meet. I am a romantic but also a realist. I feel quite content in socializing with the growing circle of friends I have made since 1981, who number in the dozens.

Since my unfortunate experiences at the Cinegay and the Bare Facts, I now have sex only with people I know well. We regularly visit each other at our homes and keep in touch by telephone at other times. I no longer panic at the idea that I may never meet "Mr. Right." These increasingly relaxed feelings about my life direction have affected my relationship with my parents for the better.

In the last eighteen months I have noticed that my parents are drinking less than they did when I was a child and a teenager. I still wish they would give up alcohol altogether, but I suspect that this is wishful thinking since they are set in their ways. From Al-Anon I learned to accept the unchangeable, and have therefore "let go" of my parents emotionally in order to allow them to make their own lives as they see fit. Since I no longer nag them about their drinking, they have become closer to me as I have to them.

We are developing a wonderful friendship.

In general I feel that I have resolved my childhood fears and discomforts. Writing this book in many successive versions over the last two years has been therapeutic, since I derive benefit from writing down my thoughts when something troubles me. Seeing my problems on the printed page gives me a sense of order and thus makes my problems less troublesome, facilitating solutions. Each revised draft of this book contained solutions for nagging problems in my life. My editor willing, this draft of "Escape from the Steel Cocoon" will be the last. If it is not, I will write the next version as a basically contented man, since the previous versions helped me to come out to myself and provide me with a sense of self-acceptance.

The original title of this book in the first draft was "Cruising" which reflected the stage of my life I was then experiencing at the Cinegay. I was a very lonely, depressed person. Now I have good friends in my life. At times I find it necessary to seek solitude in order to sort out my problems by writing this book. The time I have spent alone has been just as invaluable as the time I have spent with my friends.

I discovered that being gay is an unusual experience in terms of the proportion of gays among people in general in this world. An estimated ten percent of the human population is believed to be included in this minority. Too often gay people encounter prejudice among the people with whom we work and among those with whom we live.

Because I am not obviously effeminate, heterosexuals do not usually think I might be gay. While I worked at Skokie Realty, one of my straight colleagues told a derogatory gay joke to two other co-workers in the office; none of the three knew about my sexual orientation. Irv used the word "fag" in the joke, which made me cringe; I wanted to strangle him on the spot because of his cruel lack of tact. Instead, I went to my desk in another part of the office and kept quiet until I had regained my composure.

A few minutes later I calmly entered Irv's private office and sat down. He could see that I was troubled about something.

"Do me a favor," I told him. "Kindly tell your 'fag jokes' when I'm not around. They really bother me because I'm gay."

Irv flinched, embarrassed, and answered, "Jesus, I'm sorry Jeremy. I had no idea you were gay. I hope you didn't think I was talking about you."

"No," I said honestly. "It's just that too many straights don't try to understand gays. We're people too, you know. Thanks for listening." I stood up and left the office.

As I did so, he called out, "I really am sorry."

"It's all right," I said politely.

Irv's comment was unintentionally insulting to me. I do not resent him personally because of what he said; what I do resent is the fact that he could not appreciate the existence of all kinds of people in this world.

Many gays conceal their sexual orientation at work because of several reasons. First, they do not wish to become the target of potentially nasty gossip or direct insults. Second, some gays work in positions in which public identification with the gay lifestyle could inhibit their opportunities for advancement or even lose them their jobs altogether. Currently, no federal or state laws protect the job security of homosexuals who reveal their sexual orientation. Similarly, potential and current landlords can and do restrict housing options of men and women who openly identify themselves with the gay community. No laws protect the gay community from discriminatory property owners. (The Human Rights Ordinance passed in 1988, reversed this problem.)

Closeted homosexuals are able to circumvent such problems more easily than more visible minorities, including Blacks and Hispanics, who cannot conceal their races. Like gays who come out, Blacks and Hispanics (not to mention women) routinely face job and housing discrimination from shrewd bosses and landlords who have found ways around laws which are currently on the books and are intended to help such minorities. Closeted homosexuals routinely hide their lifestyles from their families and friends for fear of being ostracized. In extreme cases, children who came out to their families have been disinherited by parents who felt that they had somehow "failed" as mothers and fathers.

Hitler tried to exterminate the entire gay population of Europe, along with Jews, Gypsies and other "undesirable" groups. Suspected homosexuals of both sexes were sent to the gas chambers by the thousands, as part of the "Final Solution," during the Nazi reign of terror. No person suspected of being gay was brought to trial before being deported and exterminated. All suspected gays simply wore a pink triangle sewed to the uniform worn in the concentration camps, which was provided by the German army. The historic "symbol of shame" has become today's "symbol of pride" worn by some gay men and women in the nationwide Gay and Lesbian Pride Parades held every year, and on a daily basis.

Although Hitler's attempt to exterminate the gay community of Europe failed, the government of Iran today routinely stands suspected homosexuals of both sexes before firing squads in order to rid the country of *its* "problem." I understand that trials precede all such executions but that the verdict is sealed before the trial even begins.

Minorities in any country make a part of the total population. Every person, no matter what his or her background or walk in life, should be proud to acknowledge what he or she is. American tradition, however, as disseminated through movies, fairy tales, social traditions and the media, leads many people to believe that a person who differs from the majority is imperfect or wrong. (As an example, the Wicked Witch of the West, of "The Wizard of Oz" fame, was automatically feared as evil. Her ultimate death was hailed by all "good people" who believed in truth and justice as viewed by the majority.) Similarly, cowboys wearing black hats in the Westerns were considered to be evil. And, to this day, the Black community resists the stigma of "evil" and "wrong."

Until a few years ago, the American Psychiatric Association viewed homosexuality as "sick." Happily, the association realized its error. Still, one can hear stories about ultraconservative families who institutionalize their children in mental hospitals for being gay. In some extreme cases, patients are given frontal lobotomies for the purpose of easing their "mental illness." Such cases are routinely cloaked in medical verbiage which shows no apparent connection to homosexuality.

The gay community wishes that heterosexuals would understand that gays are different from straights only in the choice of sexual partners. The gay lifestyle is just as valid as the lifestyle straight people follow without qualms. Gays and straights are all people struggling to make their way in the world, deserving equal chances to succeed in employment and social settings. The world at large might think of the gay community as one reference point of several around which the world revolves.

Items on the news broadcasts concerning heterosexual rape and murder show that most people in this world do not have the answers to life. Being in the heterosexual majority does not mean that society condones the actions of its criminal element. Neither can we judge the various minorities if their activities, e.g. gay sex, do not conform to the norms of action which guide most people's lives.

I consider that it is unfair that I and my gay brothers and sisters must accept our identity and become proud of it without much verbal support from our heterosexual friends. Some heterosexuals are, however, supportive of the gay community happily, their numbers increase every day.

The two fears which I occasionally hear voiced by heterosexuals are that (a) they might be perceived as gay if they associate with men and women who openly identify themselves as gay, and that (b) their gay associates might make them or their children "queer." I can only suggest that there can be no basis for friendship between narrow-minded and open-minded heterosexuals, and that nobody can become gay from socializing with gay men and women. A person is born innately gay or straight.

I have also come across opinions to the effect that gays are "perverts." Some people reason that God is punishing gays by making them what they are. I rather believe that God made every human being without malice in mind, whatever the characteristics of the individual. I think of a slogan which I have seen printed on T-shirts and signs: "I know I'm somebody, 'cause God don't make no junk."

Accepting one's identity in life is a universal struggle. All people should realize this fact and freely offer their moral support to gay and straight people when they are "coming out." There should be equal reciprocity of emotional support for friends who need help, regardless of their sexual orientation. Once such mutual concern is routinely offered, a major step toward overall human understanding and cooperation will have been achieved.

Sadly, there are aggressive heterosexuals who hate and fear gays. In Chicago, especially during the summer, there are assaults on gay men in certain parts of the city. The victims are usually dressed in tight, short pants and "tank top" shirts (a common manner of dress adopted by less conservative gays). Such physical attacks are known in the community as "fag bashes." They are less frequent than they might be because most streetwise gay men know enough to avoid confrontations by dressing more conservatively. But such attacks still occur, causing many gay people to deny their sexual orientation for the sake of personal security. No thinking person wants to suffer injuries because of his lifestyle. Fag bashes only impede one's search for personal happiness and fulfillment as a human being.

Any search for happiness in life is a constant process, whether for gays or straights. Gays must be especially determined in their search for personal fulfillment. Everyone has regrets about one's life; mine is that I allowed my fears about homosexuality to keep me in the closet for twenty years. I suspect that the ideal time for me to have accepted myself as a homosexual would have been during college, but I will never know for certain.

I do not believe in mourning the past. I accept life as it is dealt to me rather than as it might have been. I strive to collect all the aces, and I live with the deuces that sometimes come my way. While I was coming out, I did have many moments of doubt and fear, during which I cried out to God, in anguish, "Why me, Lord?" I now know His answer. God gave me the strength and courage to be who and what I am. I praise my Maker now for having given me this gift. I have come to realize that being gay is not merely all right, but great!

I suppose that I will always have permanent scars from my experiences as a child and adolescent. I do forgive those who made my life difficult in one way or another, since they acted out of good conscience in most cases. Neither they nor I had a neatly packaged set of instructions with which to organize our lives. Everyone makes mistakes as he or she matures in life. We can only learn from those mistakes and use the experience to guide the balance of our lives.

My hopes for the future center on a unified world. I intend to do what small part I can to unify the gay and straight communities through the writing of this book and through possible public discussions with mixed audiences of heterosexuals and homosexuals. Humanity will not mature and develop as a world community without knowledge of individual parts of the whole and willingness to work together to help each other. I will probably pursue my work of bridging the gap between the gay and straight communities using the name Jeremy Simmons. I now realize that my real name is unimportant to the world at large. Only the fact that I and millions of people like me exist is important. Together we can produce a world of peace and understanding.

I believe that one needs mental and social balance in one's life. I derive such balance through an active church life (including a regular dialogue with God), regular visits with Mark and Linda, my niece and nephew, my parents, my heterosexual and homosexual friends, and my job. All of the people I have just mentioned, and people in every part of the world, have their daily concerns to handle. We must work alone and together in order to resolve any of our problems.

I hope that the readers of this book will allow themselves to see that, despite a disparity of backgrounds, our times of happiness and sadness are not too dissimilar. I have painfully faced serious childhood memories and difficult later experiences in the hope that others might benefit from the knowledge I have gained by resolving these traumas in my life.

No two people or communities can abolish all fears and prejudices which separate them unless all parties concerned are willing to listen to each other and talk with each other to the point of knowing each other's personal being. I have bared my soul publicly in an attempt to persuade other people to talk, listen and learn. Although meeting strangers can be frightening, strangers can often become friends. No two people are ever totally alike, but differences should not be obstacles to close relationships. Together we can learn about each other and, ultimately, work together to make a world in which all of us can live better than we can at present. If this book opens the door of communication between heterosexuals and homosexuals, the effort of writing it was worthwhile for the sake of its effect on people besides myself. A growing number of gays and straights routinely accept each other as *people* rather than "fags," "queers" or "dykes."

As I mature as a person I am trying to work with both the gay and the straight community. My career in real estate is my contribution to the straight community. Many families and business persons have benefited from my expertise in this field and have gone on to improve their family lives and business lives due, in some small measure, to my assistance. I am currently serving the gay community through volunteer efforts as a board member of two social organizations devoted to gay men: Mattachine Midwest and Professionals Over Thirty. I love the work I do in helping the community which gave me pride in my identity.

In short, I am a survivor. However, the story of my life is not unique. No matter how devastating the events or adverse the situations encountered in life, there is always some other person who has suffered more than we have. One may suffer terrible emotional traumas to the point of being psychologically crippled, but there is always hope. Problems can be overcome. Every human being has a spark of inborn life and the innate will to survive, traits which will carry one through the darkest hours of one's life in triumph. The negative aspects of our lives can be turned into positive ones.

We may need people along the way to help us with emotional support, counselling, understanding and redirection of our lives. Primarily, one must be willing to consider alternatives to the way he or she is currently living. If we are open to the possibility of change in our lives, and if we believe that things can get better, we can do anything.

I took an important first step in improving my life when I discovered that I must take charge of my own life and accept responsibility for my own actions. The rest of my life was made easier because of that first step.

I believe that, in order for a person to be truly happy, he or she must decide that mere existence is not enough. Decide to be happy and fulfilled emotionally. Realize that such a task is not only possible but worthy of yourself. Only then the journey toward attainment of one's true self at last can be the most exciting and rewarding experience any person will ever have. Everyone owes it to himself or herself to make the effort. Good luck!

POSTSCRIPT

I finished writing "Escape" five years ago. I am now forty and a recovering drug addict and alcoholic. It took five years to get ready to accept myself as I was and am now and to publish this book.

Many people besides Russ Ford and Susan Filler (the people who I dedicate the work) have helped. Certainly they were important in keeping me on the road to recovery and self acceptance.

My literary agent today is Paul Samuelson. He has tirelessly inspired and guided me in the creation of the final draft.

Tim Basaldua, of Automated Graphics, spent days processing the manuscript and formatting the pages. He also introduced me to the book "Literary Marketplace", an invaluable tool for writers.

Also, I wish to thank my proofreader, Carol McGury. Without her wise and attentive help, the narrative would not have flowed as accurately and as well as it did.

Finally, I have my illustrator and graphic designer to thank for their dramatically appealing cover of this book. They asked me not to use their names. I won't let the book go to print, however, without acknowledging my gratitude for their invaluable work.

It's a humbling experience for me to live a life where I thought I had many of life's answers, only to discover I need and want so much more help and loving advice to put the pieces together. I discover it's what I learned after I knew it all that really counts.

I'm very grateful to *all* my friends.

www.ingramcontent.com/pod-product-compliance
Lightning Source LLC
Chambersburg PA
CBHW061315280526
45784CB00002B/989